INVISIBLE BARRIERS TACKLING UNCONSCIOUS BIAS IN THE WORKPLACE, LEADERS AND ORGANISATION

BY: PETER JOHNSON

© **Copyright 2025, Peter Johnson**

All rights reserved. No part of this publication may be reproduced, distributed, or transmitted in any form or by any means, including photocopying, recording, or other electronic or mechanical methods, without the prior written permission of the publisher, except in the case of brief quotations embodied in critical reviews and certain other noncommercial uses permitted by copyright law.

First Printing edition 2025.

TABLE OF CONTENTS

INTRODUCTION 5

    DEFINING UNCONSCIOUS BIAS 5

PART I: UNDERSTANDING UNCONSCIOUS BIAS 13

    THE SCIENCE OF BIAS 13

    HOW THE BRAIN FORMS BIASES 13

    TYPES OF UNCONSCIOUS BIAS 15

    THE IMPACT OF BIAS 19

    THE HISTORICAL CONTEXT 27

PART II: RECOGNIZING BIAS IN YOUR WORKPLACE 36

    IDENTIFYING BIAS IN ORGANIZATIONAL PROCESSES 36

    THE ROLE OF DATA IN ADDRESSING BIAS 69

    THE POWER OF HUMANIZING DATA 77

    PERSONAL REFLECTION 79

PART III: ADDRESSING AND REDUCING BIAS 93

    CREATING AN INCLUSIVE CULTURE 93

    STRATEGIES FOR PROMOTING EQUITY 107

    LEADERSHIP'S ROLE 131

    INTERVENTIONS THAT WORK 135

PART IV: MOVING FORWARD: MEASURING SUCCESS IN DIVERSITY, EQUITY, AND INCLUSION (DEI) 147

    THE ROLE OF TECHNOLOGY IN DIVERSITY, EQUITY, AND INCLUSION (DEI) 196

    SUSTAINING CHANGE 217

PART V: BUILDING LONG-TERM COMMITMENT TO DIVERSITY AND INCLUSION 249

    EMBEDDING BIAS REDUCTION INTO ORGANIZATIONAL STRATEGY 249

    ENGAGING EMPLOYEES IN THE DEI JOURNEY 283

    LEADERSHIP DEVELOPMENT FOR INCLUSIVE LEADERSHIP 313

    BUILDING A DIVERSE TALENT PIPELINE 342

    LEGAL AND ETHICAL CONSIDERATIONS 347

PART VI: OVERCOMING ORGANIZATIONAL CHALLENGES 374

    ALIGNING DEI WITH ORGANIZATIONAL CULTURE 377

ADDRESSING INTERSECTIONALITY IN THE WORKPLACE 389

PART VII: SCALING AND EXPANDING DEI INITIATIVES 392

COLLABORATIVE PARTNERSHIPS AND COMMUNITY ENGAGEMENT 397

LEVERAGING EXTERNAL FEEDBACK 399

A VISION FOR THE FUTURE 404

CONCLUSION 408

INTRODUCTION

DEFINING UNCONSCIOUS BIAS

Unconscious bias describes the mental shortcuts or automatic judgments we make about people based on stereotypes, beliefs, or experiences without our conscious intention. These biases operate beneath the conscious awareness and very often influence how we interact, perceive, and make decisions. For instance, you may unconsciously favor candidates who remind you of people you have previously worked with, or you may believe that certain jobs are better suited for a particular gender or ethnic group. This can lead to unequal opportunities, whereby individuals with particular characteristics, such as race, gender, age, or background, are excluded or marginalized.

The unconscious bias will affect everyday interactions, such as making judgments about fellow colleagues, judging their performances, or simply guessing their potential. You might make unconscious attributions regarding personality traits or leadership qualities to others based on looks or backgrounds and may continue to treat them unequally because of that. These acts are contributors toward developing a work environment that will not tap into the actual power of diversity and promote missed opportunities for growth and inclusion.

In addition, unconscious bias may affect decision-making regarding hiring, promotion, or project assignment. A manager may give preference to an individual unconsciously because the individual reminds him of himself or a person he trusts, overlooking equally qualified candidates who don't fit the mold. This builds on a cycle of exclusion and limited perspectives detrimental to an organization's overall success and innovation.

Identifying these biases is the first step toward addressing them since they usually remain hidden unless examined and challenged. Understanding how these biases work will help us build more equitable practices that support diversity and inclusion in the workplace.

Its Origins in Psychology and Neuroscience

Unconscious bias has a deep root in psychology, where humans are wired to categorize and simplify large amounts of information in order to make sense of the world. Our brains are designed to process information quickly through two primary systems:

System 1 refers to automatic, intuitive thinking while

System 2 refers to slower, more deliberate thinking. Life experience, social norms, and cultural conditioning inform the automatic, fast decisions of System 1. These are the bases of unconscious bias.

Neuroscience helps a little more. Biases are formed mainly in the unconscious part of the brain, including key regions such as the amygdala and prefrontal cortex. The amygdala is responsible for much of the processing of emotional reactions; it commonly provokes fear, familiarity, or discomfort in unusual situations. This is the reason it leads to instinctive, automatic acting based on former experiences or stereotypes. Meanwhile, the prefrontal cortex, responsible for rational, complex thinking, overrules these biases in deliberate and controlled decisions, but in the absence of focused attention, the amygdala dominates, and unconscious bias takes place.

This interplay of the emotive and cognitive parts of the brain produces automatic judgments based on familiarity, comfort, and cultural norms. For example, in hiring, a person may unconsciously favor these types of candidates over others with whom they have had previous experience rather than making an objective judgment about who is best qualified for the position. These biases, normally developed over many years, are inculcated deeply and influence both large-scale organizational practices and day-to-day interactions.

This neural process explains, on the one hand, why unconscious bias is hard to detect and change. Still, on the other hand, it points to awareness and intervention as necessary steps in creating an inclusive environment. By recognizing the interplay between the brain's emotional and cognitive systems, individuals and organizations can mitigate these biases and foster greater diversity and fairness.

Why It Matters in the Workplace

Unconscious bias strongly influences hiring, promotions, team dynamics, and day-to-day interactions within a workplace. It may lead to unfair or inconsistent decisions. For example, it may cause hiring managers to pass on qualified candidates for not fitting into the mental "ideal" image in their minds and thus discourage diversity. This not only limits the pool of talent but also hampers innovation, since diverse teams outperform homogeneous groups due to bringing a wider range of perspectives and experiences to bear on the discussion.

Moreover, unconscious bias engenders a culture of favor and exclusion in which some groups of employees feel overlooked or marginalized. Employees not valued due to bias may experience disengagement, lower morale, and reduced productivity. This inevitably leads to higher turnover rates over time as employees leave in search of workplaces where they are recognized and valued.

Moreover, biased decisions also lead to missed opportunities for career advancement. For instance, employees in underrepresented groups may not be promoted despite their capabilities and qualifications for holding certain positions. This lack of advancement affects not only individuals but also organizations, which are deprived of the special talents and insights these employees would provide.

On the other hand, a workplace without unconscious bias provides equity, innovation, and inclusiveness in culture. When employees feel valued and respected, they are more likely to be better engaged, motivated, and committed to their work. A diverse and inclusive workforce nurtures fresh ideas, collaboration, and creative problem-solving skills, leading to organizational success. Embracing diversity allows the avenue to be open for all to prosper, hence allowing great outcomes both individually and at an organizational level.

The Impact on Organizational Success

Organizations that address unconscious bias often see better performance, higher creativity, and increased employee satisfaction. When teams' welcome diversity, they combine a great deal of experience, background, and perspectives that foster collaboration and bring about better problem-solving and decision-making. The research proves that diverse teams are more creative because they attack challenges from different angles, explore new ideas, and are more likely to discover unique opportunities that others might miss.

Unconscious bias, however, may lead to groupthink-similar perspectives that dominate and leave little room for creative thinking and fresh solutions. When people like themselves surround individuals, they may fail to recognize essential insights or reject innovative ideas simply because those ideas feel unfamiliar or uncomfortable. By minimizing bias, organizations create an environment in which diverse voices are welcome, respected, and valued, and a healthier exchange of ideas can take place – one that leads to better results.

In addition, a workplace that effectively reduces unconscious bias tends to have higher levels of employee satisfaction and engagement. When employees feel that their contributions are valued, regardless of their background, they are most likely motivated and productive in focusing on the organization's goals. Inclusive environments foster a sense of belonging that heightens well-being, lowers turnover, and fortifies loyalty to the organization.

Decreasing unconscious bias is not a question of being fair but creating a workplace that is agile, resilient, and able to thrive in today's diverse world. Organizations that prioritize inclusion and equity will be better positioned to attract top talent, build strong leadership, and foster a work culture reflective of their values and long-term objectives. Addressing unconscious bias ensures organizational success by fostering an enabling, inclusive, and sustainable future.

Objectives of the Book

The main goal of this book is to equip you with the knowledge and tools to identify and challenge unconscious bias in the workplace. By understanding how these biases affect your decisions, you'll gain the ability to make more inclusive choices. You'll explore practical strategies, including ways to build self-awareness, foster open communication, and create a supportive work environment where diversity is valued. Additionally, we will examine real-world examples of bias and provide actionable steps to help individuals and organizations cultivate equity, respect, and fairness.

By the end of this book, you'll be empowered to take steps that promote inclusive practices, mitigate bias, and contribute to a more equitable and productive workplace.

PART I: UNDERSTANDING UNCONSCIOUS BIAS

THE SCIENCE OF BIAS

Unconscious bias refers to judgments, preferences, or assumptions we make without realizing it. These biases are often shaped by our experiences, upbringing, and the environment around us. They operate beneath the surface of our conscious awareness and influence our behavior, attitudes, and decision-making.

HOW THE BRAIN FORMS BIASES

Our brains are wired to simplify and process vast amounts of information quickly to help us navigate the world efficiently. However, this can lead to biases as a form of mental shortcut.

- **Cognitive Processing**: Our brain uses mental shortcuts called heuristics to make quick decisions. While these shortcuts help us save time and energy, they sometimes lead to biased judgments.

- **Availability Heuristic**: This bias occurs when we judge the likelihood of events based on how easily examples come to mind, often leading to overgeneralizations. For instance, if we frequently hear about certain negative behaviors associated with a group, we may assume that all members of that group are the same.

- **Experience & Exposure**: Our past experiences, cultural background, and the people we interact with contribute to how we view the world and the assumptions we make about others.

- **Cultural Influence**: Different cultural environments shape our values, beliefs, and norms, which can contribute to unconscious biases. For example, suppose someone grows up in a culture that values certain traits over others (like collectivism vs. individualism). In that case, they may develop biased preferences for certain types of behavior or people.

- **Social Interactions**: The people we frequently engage with, whether through family, friends, or colleagues, can reinforce or challenge our biases. Over time, repeated exposure to certain groups or individuals can strengthen or weaken these biases.

TYPES OF UNCONSCIOUS BIAS

1. **Affinity Bias**: We tend to feel more connected or favorable toward people who are similar to us (e.g., people of the same race, gender, or background). This can lead to favoritism in hiring decisions, promotions, or social interactions, creating an environment where diversity is undervalued or overlooked.

    - **In the Workplace**, recruiters may gravitate toward candidates who remind them of themselves, unintentionally excluding qualified candidates from underrepresented groups.
    - **In Social Settings**, we tend to build stronger relationships with people who share our values, habits, or backgrounds, reinforcing homogeneous groups.

2. **Confirmation Bias**: We seek information that confirms our preexisting beliefs and ignore

information that contradicts them. This tendency to filter out facts or viewpoints that challenge our assumptions leads to a narrower perspective.

- **Decision-Making**: In professional settings, managers might overlook diverse opinions that don't align with their existing beliefs, which can hinder innovation and limit creativity.

- **Personal Relationships**: People often interpret information in ways that support their preconceived notions, reinforcing misunderstandings and perpetuating biases.

3. **Stereotyping** is when we apply generalizations or assumptions about a group of people based on characteristics like race, gender, or age without considering individual differences.

- **Social Impact**: Stereotypes can contribute to inequality by shaping how we perceive others' abilities, behaviors, and roles. For example, assumptions about who should lead in a particular field (e.g., women in leadership roles or men in caregiving roles) can limit opportunities.

- **Media and Culture**: Media representations often reinforce stereotypes, portraying certain groups in limited or biased ways, perpetuating a cycle of misinformation.

The Link Between Stereotypes and Bias

Stereotypes are inaccurate or unfair beliefs about groups of people. Unconscious biases often stem from these stereotypes, influencing how we perceive and interact with others.

- **Generalizations vs. Reality**: Stereotypes oversimplify complex human characteristics and behaviors, often ignoring individual differences. For example, assuming all people of a certain race, gender, or background behave the same way can lead to false conclusions.

- **Self-Fulfilling Prophecy**: Once we hold certain stereotypes, we may act in ways that reinforce them, creating a feedback loop. For example, if a manager assumes a certain group is less capable of leadership, they might overlook those individuals for promotions, leading to fewer opportunities and reinforcing the stereotype.

Example: If you believe that "all men are good at math," this stereotype can lead to biased expectations in educational settings or the workplace. A teacher might have lower expectations for female students in math, or a manager may be more likely to assign leadership roles to men, even when qualified women are available.

Impact on Opportunity

These biases can shape how we treat people and make decisions about hiring, promotions, and even our day-to-day interactions.

- **Hiring and Promotions**: Biases can lead to discrimination in recruitment, where candidates are evaluated unfairly based on stereotypes rather than qualifications.
- **Workplace Dynamics**: They can contribute to the underrepresentation of certain groups in leadership positions, hindering diversity and innovation.

- **Everyday Interactions**: Unconscious bias can lead to microaggressions, where people unknowingly make dismissive or derogatory comments based on stereotypes, affecting how individuals feel valued and respected.

Understanding the science of bias helps us recognize how these hidden patterns shape our behavior, paving the way to reducing their influence.

THE IMPACT OF BIAS

Bias can influence important workplace decisions like recruitment, promotions, and performance reviews. Understanding its impact is crucial for fostering a more inclusive and equitable environment.

Case Studies of Bias in Recruitment, Promotions, and Performance Reviews

- **Recruitment Bias**

Often comes in the form of unconscious bias for candidates who "fit the mold" of their present culture. For instance, if a company has been used to valuing certain qualifications, certain educational backgrounds, or industry experience, it is likely to overlook highly qualified candidates who come from other different backgrounds. These people can bring in unique insight, fresh ideas, and valuable experiences not represented by the current pool of employees at the company.

Different studies show that biases based on gender, race, age, and even educational background are barriers to qualified candidates joining. For example, females and people of color face significant challenges in recruitment processes due to unconscious biases about the "fit" of women and colored people in the job. This often eventually leads to a lack of diversity within teams, hindering innovation and company performance in the long run.

Moreover, diverse teams exhibit better performance and contribute significantly to higher levels of creativity and problem-solving. By neglecting candidates from underrepresented groups, companies forfeit the very talent that could drive those outcomes and eventually impede growth and progress.

- **Promotion Bias**

Bias during promotions is another critical area where unconscious preferences can have significant impacts. Managers may unconsciously favor employees who resemble themselves or who embody characteristics they perceive as "ideal" for leadership roles. These biases often stem from assumptions about what makes a leader successful, which may favor traits traditionally associated with dominant or majority groups.

For instance, women and minority candidates may be overlooked for leadership roles due to biases around perceived competence, leadership style, or even communication patterns. Research has shown that behaviors such as assertiveness or confidence are often viewed differently based on gender or cultural background. For example, women who exhibit assertiveness may be perceived as "too aggressive," while similar behavior in men is often seen as leadership potential.

Similarly, minority candidates may be subject to stereotypes about their qualifications or suitability for specific roles. This can lead to their exclusion from leadership pipelines, resulting in underrepresentation at senior levels. As a result, organizations lose out on the benefits of diverse leadership, which include better decision-making, increased creativity, and a broader understanding of different perspectives.

The underrepresentation of women and minority groups in leadership roles not only limits access to career advancement opportunities for these groups but also reduces the overall diversity of leadership teams. Organizations that fail to address these biases may miss out on the potential benefits of diverse leadership, such as improved innovation, increased employee engagement, and better overall business outcomes.

- **Performance Reviews Bias**

Performance reviews, meant to be objective assessments of employee contributions, are prone to bias. One area where this can occur is in managers' evaluations of their employees. For example, managers may have subjective preferences for an individual's traits, such as confidence, assertiveness, or style of communication. These subjective preferences lead to biased evaluations.

As a result, the more vocal or dominantly communicative workers are highly rated, while the quiet or less conventionally "assertive" colleagues remain undervalued. This is most true for female and minority workers, who are typically socialized to develop other styles of communicating that do not fit in with traditional notions of leadership.

Research has surfaced that proves bias in communication style and behavior makes certain employees either underperform or be less valued because they do not fit the mold of what managers perceive as a "high performer." For instance, very often, women and minorities are judged on stereotypes about how they should behave or interact at work, and that leads to unfair assessments and overlooks promotion or growth opportunities.

Moreover, managers tend to have biases regarding perceived "cultural fit" or personality trait prejudices, further muddying performance reviews. This makes them even less objective and closes out much-needed employees who will lead an organization toward better results.

The Cost of Bias on Innovation, Employee Morale, and Retention

- **Innovation suffered**

Bias cuts down the scope of ideas that shall be considered valuable. Teams made up of people who think similarly, or who come from similar backgrounds, are not apt to challenge the status quo. This homogeneity creates an echo chamber in which the perspectives of a few dominate discussion and options, thus limiting creativity and reducing the chances of finding a breakthrough idea.

Diverse teams, on the other hand, carry with them wide experiences, backgrounds, and viewpoints, so important for driving innovation. They are more likely to look at problems from a different angle, question assumptions, and investigate unofficial solutions. When biased and not fully contributing diverse teams make organizations blind to the opportunities of innovation and evolution.

Moreover, innovation tends to thrive in places where people feel safe in presenting their various thoughts. The contributions are usually dismissed or overlooked if certain groups feel ostracized or marginalized by the biases in recruitments, promotions, or performance appraisals. In turn, this suppresses several valuable insights and correspondingly fewer instances of creative breakthroughs.

- **Employee Morale Takes a Hit**

When employees perceive bias in recruitment, promotions, or performance reviews, there is a great setback to the morale of workers. Thus, workers-especially underrepresented groups-may feel not being valued or heard. All this results in detachment from work, reduced satisfaction with one's job, and isolation from other staff members.

Bias erodes trust in fairness within the organization and builds a work environment in which employees feel that their contributions are not valued. High-performing employees who feel that they have been passed over because of a bias may become disenchanted, leading to decreased morale, lower productivity, and increased turnover. Workplaces that foster fairness and equity tend to engender higher morale, greater trust, and stronger commitment to the organization.

- **Retention Problems**

Bias impacts employee retention, particularly for women, minorities, and other underrepresented groups. In instances where employees feel their chances for growth are being severely limited or blocked through biased practice, they tend to migrate elsewhere for a place to work. High turnover raises the costs associated with recruiting and training new employees, which diminishes team cohesion and general organizational stability.

Lack of diversity in the senior level further leads to a different message wherein certain groups are not appreciated, which drives away the pool of qualified talent. Such organizations that cannot retain their best performing lot due to biases in their systems will thus continue to suffer from this vicious cycle of underperformance and talent drain.

Leadership Diversity and Organizational Success

Diverse leadership has been associated with many other benefits, including increased profitability, better decision-making, and even higher levels of employee satisfaction. Bias-free recruitment, promotion, and performance review systems allow people from underrepresented groups to rise into leadership positions, fostering more inclusive environments where diverse perspectives are valued and actively leveraged.

Organizations that appreciate diversity at all levels of their workings create an inclusive and innovative environment. Where organizations build equitable practices by getting rid of bias, the result should be trust in the workforce and high morale for employees toward organizational success. Diverse teams can come up with innovative solutions that ensure continuous growth and a sustained competitive advantage.

Conclusion

Biases in recruitment, promotions, and performance reviews not only impact individual employees but also have broader organizational effects. By addressing these biases, companies can improve morale, boost innovation, and enhance retention, fostering a more inclusive and productive workplace. The key is to create awareness, implement fair practices, and cultivate an environment that values diverse perspectives.

THE HISTORICAL CONTEXT

Workplace bias is not an isolated issue but a systemic problem deeply rooted in a long history of societal and cultural factors. To fully comprehend its impact, we must delve into the complex web of influences that have shaped it over time.

How Systemic Inequality Shapes Workplace Bias

Systemic inequality, the foundation of deeply ingrained disparities within society's structures like education, wealth distribution, and legal systems, is a key driver of workplace biases. These inequalities manifest in various ways, affecting opportunities and outcomes for specific groups.

- **Access to Opportunities**

Historically, marginalized communities have had limited access to quality education and professional networks. This lack of access creates a "pipeline problem," where fewer individuals from these groups are positioned for high-paying or leadership roles. As a result, employers often see a workforce that doesn't reflect the diversity of the wider population.

- **Stereotypes Reinforced Over Time**

Systemic inequality fosters stereotype that creep into hiring, promotions, and evaluations. For example, biases may assume men are better leaders or women are less committed due to family responsibilities. These stereotypes aren't born overnight—generations of unequal treatment shape them.

- **The Pay Gap and Unequal Representation**

Disparities in pay and representation are both symptoms and causes of systemic inequality. Women and minorities often earn less and hold fewer leadership positions, which reinforces a cycle of undervaluation.

Human Impact:

Think of the single mother of two who is equally qualified but has to struggle to get a promotion because she's perceived as "less available." Assumptions about her personal life overshadow her hard work, long hours, and innovative ideas. Or the young Black professional who gets passed over for leadership training because no one in the leadership team "looks like him," leaving him to wonder if his contributions will ever be indeed recognized. These are not just numbers; these are stories of real people whose talents and ambitions are stifled.

Consider the brilliant young woman in STEM who consistently outperforms her peers but has never been given projects-repeatedly passed over-rewarded to her male colleagues because they seem, by default, to hold positions of "more capability as leaders." Think about that LGBTQ+ employee who decides that coming into work daily authentic to themselves may make others uncomfortable or hurt their chances with possible career advancement. Or the middle-aged worker whose good experience and skills are belittled because such a person is considered "out of touch" in a young man's world.

Bias doesn't stop at blocking opportunities-it erodes confidence, builds resentment, and drives talented people out of their fields altogether. It is not just the individuals who suffer; organizations lose out on innovation, diverse perspectives, and the full potential of their workforce. When real people face these barriers, the ripple effects extend into communities, perpetuating inequality.

Each overlooked promotion, each discounted idea, and each suppressed voice adds another layer to this multifaceted problem. These are not isolated incidents but are part of a larger system we need to fix. It's crucial that we approach this task with empathy, understanding the human impact of bias and the need for change.

The Role of Culture and Society

Culture and societal norms play a significant role in shaping workplace dynamics. What we believe about work, leadership, and success is influenced by the values and behaviors normalized around us. Here's how culture and society reinforce workplace bias:

- **Gender Roles in Society**

Traditional gender roles often dictate what is "appropriate" for men and women. For instance, society may expect women to be nurturing and men to be assertive. In the workplace, these norms translate into biases, such as the assumption that women are better suited for support roles while men excel in leadership.

- **Cultural Attitudes Toward Authority**

In some cultures, respect for authority may discourage employees from marginalized backgrounds from challenging unfair practices or speaking up about biases. This silence can perpetuate inequality and make systemic bias harder to dismantle.

- **Media and Representation**

Media often portrays certain groups in stereotypical ways, which influences societal perceptions and workplace interactions. For example, the underrepresentation of women and minorities in media leadership roles can subconsciously suggest that such positions are "not for them."

- **The "Cultural Fit" Myth**

Many organizations hire based on "cultural fit," which can be code for replicating existing team dynamics. This approach often excludes individuals who bring unique perspectives but don't match the dominant group's background or style.

Human Impact:

Picture a young woman in tech who feels isolated by the men occupying every leadership position, subtly signaling that she does not belong there. She goes to meetings where her ideas are discussed until she hears them praised when they have been repeated by male colleagues. Over time, such exclusion eats away at her confidence and makes her question her place in an industry she once felt passionate about.

Or think of an immigrant employee whose accents lead colleagues to underestimate his abilities. Despite his problem-solving and deliverance, he isn't called for client-facing work because others have made poor assumptions concerning his communication skills. Every missed opportunity cement that his contributions are somehow "less valid."

Now, imagine an older employee in a fast-paced startup who is excluded from brainstorming sessions because they're seen as "outdated" or "slow to adapt." Their years of experience and wisdom, which could provide invaluable insights, are sidelined in favor of younger voices that align with the company's perceived image of innovation.

Consider the nonbinary individual who avoids disclosing their pronouns at work, fearing judgment or alienation. Each slip-up in recognition has the silent effect of disavowing their identity altogether, as they must learn to work their way through an unreceptive and sometimes even hostile place of employment.

These are not isolated experiences but realities lived by many in workplaces ingrained with cultural conditioning. These daily struggles build environments where inclusion feels more like an afterthought than an action priority. They become barriers to innovation, collaboration, and growth for individuals and organizations alike.

By acknowledging these struggles and roots of cultural conditioning, the path can be paved to workplaces where everyone feels valued, respected, and empowered to thrive. This commitment to diversity and inclusion is not just a goal, but a necessity for creating truly equitable and innovative workplaces.

Why This Matters

Understanding the historical context of workplace bias isn't about pointing fingers—it's about recognizing how society has shaped the systems we operate in today. By acknowledging these influences, we can take active steps to break the cycle and create workplaces that value everyone for their unique contributions. The urgency of this task cannot be overstated, and it's up to each of us to take responsibility and act.

PART II: RECOGNIZING BIAS IN YOUR WORKPLACE

IDENTIFYING BIAS IN ORGANIZATIONAL PROCESSES

Bias is often subtle but can significantly influence workplace dynamics, decision-making, and overall employee satisfaction. To create an inclusive and equitable environment, it's essential to recognize and address biases embedded in organizational processes. Let's break this down:

Recruitment and Hiring

Bias in recruitment and hiring can hinder diversity and limit an organization's potential. Unconscious preferences or assumptions can creep into the hiring process, even when intentions are good. Let's take a closer look at how this happens and actionable ways to address it.

Resume Screening

- **Name-Based Bias**

Name-based bias in recruitment is one of the more insidious, yet pervasive, issues undermining fairness in hiring processes. Time and again, research has demonstrated that candidates with ethnic-sounding or non-Western names often receive fewer callbacks, even when their qualifications are identical to people with more familiar or Westernized names. This may be a function of unconscious associations that recruiters make between certain names and stereotypes about a person's competence, education, or cultural fit.

This is further exacerbated by a natural tendency to orient toward what is familiar. Recruiters may unconsciously be drawn to names with which they are familiar or can easily pronounce, reflecting the similarity-attraction dynamic. This leads to perfectly qualified candidates falling through selection cracks simply because their surnames don't meet some preconceived expectations. In extreme cases, people feel compelled to modify or anglicize their names on resumes in order to be considered for jobs; this is absolutely a case of systemic inequity.

The solution to this problem is quite proactive. Some of the best ways include anonymizing resumes, such that except for qualifications and experience, everything else like the name is removed during the initial screenings. Another method could be making hiring managers aware of their unconscious bias, which would help them make more equitable decisions. Organizations benefit a lot from elimination of name-based bias as it opens more avenues for talent, increases their reputation as inclusive employers, and builds teams promoting innovation and creativity.

Therefore, the shift of focus away from names to skills enables corporations to incorporate a process that champions both potential and contribution over mere familiarity, hence being non-discriminatory for all candidates.

- **Education Bias**

Another bias that leads to poor diversity and talent is the over-emphasis on recruiting people from prestigious schools. It may be true that the graduate of an elite school exhibits a certain level of academic ability, but it does not necessarily translate into the greatest abilities, potential, or real-world performance. There are plenty of talents who, because of opportunity or resources, were never able to go to these schools and who possess equal-if not greater-abilities that have not been tapped due to this bias.

This is usually based on the assumption that candidates from prestigious schools are innately more capable or better trained. However, such assumptions short-sight critical factors such as personal drive, resilience, and hands-on experience, which often outweigh the benefits of an elite education. What's more, giving priority to prestigious institutions reinforces socioeconomic inequality since these schools are mostly accessible only to those with substantial financial means or a privileged background.

The organizations pay a price for this narrow approach to academic pedigree: it limits the talent pool and closes out many people who would bring diverse perspectives and different problem-solving approaches. These individuals often bring creativity, adaptability, and a strong work ethic forged through their nontraditional journeys.

Better results can be achieved by making a shift in hiring skills, achievements, and potential rather than the name of the school. Tools like skills-based assessments, work samples, and structured interviews help identify candidates that best fit the needs of the organization, regardless of educational background.

This opens a wider perspective that enables companies to foster an inclusive culture and create teams rich in diversity and innovation-teams that will drive success long into the future.

- **Career Gaps**

The most common error in recruitment practices is the automatic penalization of applicants with employment gaps, which is a highly fallible practice. Employment gaps are often viewed as red flags, indicating a lack of commitment, skills, or reliability. However, such a presumption completely disregards the varied and valid reasons people step away from work: caregiving responsibilities, further education, maintenance of personal health, or even taking a career sabbatical to re-evaluate goals and priorities.

For example, caregiving is a job that is both necessary and undervalued, requiring skills of organization, problem-solving, and multitasking-skills highly transferable to the workplace. Similarly, pursuing additional education or certification during a career interruption shows growth and a desire to learn. Without considering these experiences, the broader context of an applicant's life and the potential skill acquisition during their time away from traditional employment are being dismissed.

Moreover, such penalizing gaps disproportionately affect women-for instance, in childcare-and particular groups facing systemic barriers. It often inadvertently promotes inequality and depletes a potential pool of candidates with much-needed perspectives and talents for organizations.

Instead, the more inclusive mindset would be taken as one where the breaks in employment are viewed as neutral rather than inherently bad. Recruiters could have more substantive conversations with candidates about their career journeys and explore how their experiences align with the requirements of the role. Open-ended questions about what they learned or achieved during their time away may uncover hidden strengths and insight that will benefit the organization.

It finally allows organizations to reframe how they think about job gaps and build out teams that value qualities such as resilience, adaptability, and the various routes individuals take to success. Moving beyond rigid assumptions cultivates a more equitable hiring process and unlocks a broader spectrum of talent.

- **Experience Inflation**

Overemphasis on years of experience over relevant skills in a position is the general bias that unjustly sets younger candidates or career changers at a disadvantage. While experience often measures time spent in the respective field, it does not necessarily equate to competence, adaptability, or indeed the ability to excel at a particular role. This bias reinforces the notion that career length is a better determinant of success than the kind of skills one brings on board or even their potential to grow and contribute.

Younger candidates, though less experienced in professional fields, possess fresh ideas, updated knowledge, and technological fluency. They probably excel in collaboration, creativity, and the ability to learn new tools and processes fast. Similarly, career-switchers often bring an extensive collection of transferable skills, fresh outlooks, and experiences from other sectors, which further enrich the approach of a team when it comes to solving problems or creating innovative approaches.

It would also blind the organizations to age bias by overemphasizing years of experience and excluding a huge pool of talented individuals. This could also deter a lot of qualified candidates from applying because they may not be able to meet arbitrary thresholds of experience, even when they can fully perform their job duties.

Better still is to give precedence to relevant skills, demonstrated achievements, and a candidate's ability to adapt and learn. Structured hiring, incorporating skills assessments, practical exercises, or scenario-based interviews, will provide a more accurate indication of a candidate's potential. Moreover, valuing a mix of experienced professionals and newer entrants will create balanced teams where institutional knowledge complements fresh perspectives.

Ultimately, this shifts the focus from years of experience to relevant capabilities, making it inclusive, ensuring a wider talent pool, and allowing organizations to tap into the unique strengths of each candidate, regardless of career stage. This approach fosters not only fairness but also innovation and long-term success.

What You Can Do:

- Use applicant tracking systems (ATS) that anonymize personal details during the screening process.

- Focus on skill-based assessments rather than heavily relying on traditional resumes.

Job Descriptions

- **Language Matters**

Language is a powerful driver of perception, and if a word or phrase is used in a job description, it may well act to discourage applications from underrepresented groups. For example, words like "aggressive" or "ninja," meant to indicate ambition or specialized skill, may have unintended consequences. Such words align with traditionally masculine stereotypes, potentially discouraging women or those who don't identify with the trait from applying. This narrows the talent pool and perpetuates a homogenous workforce.

Similarly, wordings like "native English speaker" may inadvertently eliminate multilingual candidates who could be very proficient in the language and bring so much cross-cultural experience. These candidates are often highly competent communicators with the ability to navigate diverse environments, which is an asset in today's globalized workplace. Such wording may connote bias-even when unintended-and serve as barriers to otherwise qualified individuals who would excel in the position.

Inclusive language attracts a diverse pool of candidates. Using such words as "collaborative," "innovative," or "skilled communicator" describes behaviors and skills desired without relying on stereotypes and creating unwarranted exclusions. Job descriptions should not use overly complicated or jargon-heavy language that intimidates and alienates candidates from underrepresented backgrounds who may have not been exposed to specific terminologies, yet could possess the capabilities.

Besides, providing alternative qualifications or emphasizing flexibility, such as "proficiency in English" instead of "native English speaker," can be a signal of an inclusive approach. This opens opportunities for multilingual candidates to show their unique strengths, which often include adaptability, problem-solving, and cultural awareness.

Thus, by choosing words with a lot of care and framing the descriptions in job posts as inclusive, organizations create space where diversified candidates would love to come aboard, which helps not only to increase the talent pool but also its variety. Inclusive language isn't about avoiding exclusion; it is about fostering a culture that makes everyone feel included.

- **Qualifications Overload**

Loading a job description with a long list of "preferred" qualifications is likely to have an unintentional effect of discouraging underrepresented groups from applying, even when they meet the core requirements. Research has shown that candidates from marginalized groups, especially women and those coming from minority backgrounds, are more likely to self-select out of the application process if they don't meet every listed qualification. This behavior is resultant of systemic factors, among them imposter syndrome and the societal norms that push these groups to feel they must exceed expectations if they are to be considered.

For example, a job description that contains an exhaustive list of preferred qualifications-such as extensive amounts of degrees, certifications, or special experience-may be suggesting to candidates that they need all the requirements to be considered. This might prevent highly competent individuals with many valuable skills, experiences, and perspectives from applying when they are actually meeting or exceeding the essential qualifications for the position.

On the other hand, stressing qualifications too much also bolsters unconscious biases among hiring teams. If a panel focuses too much on such "extras," they subconsciously favor candidates from higher backgrounds who had more privilege to educational or professional opportunities, extending workplace inequality.

To this end, clarity of and inclusivity around the actual job posting, such that "must-have" qualifications are separated from "nice-to-have"-the latter few and truly optional-emphasize valuing transferable skills; highlight the organization's commitment to hiring candidates with different experiences and perspectives. Phrasing such as "If you meet most of these qualifications, we encourage you to apply" assures candidates that they will be considered holistically.

In a much more streamlined and inclusive manner, this approach broadens the talent pool, increases equity, and allows organizations to uncover remarkable candidates who might otherwise have been overlooked. By focusing on what really matters for the role, companies can build dynamic, innovative, and representative teams.

What You Can Do:

- Use gender-neutral language and tools like job description analyzers to identify and eliminate biased terms.

- Emphasize a growth mindset in your postings by highlighting opportunities for learning and development.

Interview Panels

- **Lack of Representation**

Homogenous panels, comprising people from similar backgrounds, experiences, and viewpoints, could be unconsciously propagating biased judgments in the selection process. When panels are homogenous, they are much more susceptible to groupthink, or prioritizing consensus and familiar perspectives over diverse and innovative approaches. This may exclude candidates whose experiences, ideas, and contributions might differ from those of the panel members.

Candidates from underrepresented backgrounds may not feel welcome or connected if they are interacting with a very homogeneous panel. This is a recipe for exclusion, and it reduces confidence-which diminishes the likeliness of a candidate's performing their best in an interview setup. People naturally are more likely to feel comfortable and connected with others who are like themselves-research proves this-and more subtle biases toward candidates who look like them, or think like them, will manifest themselves.

To mitigate these issues, the organizations should always try to make the interview panel as diverse as possible. A mix of genders, cultural backgrounds, professional experiences, and perspectives will bring a wide range of insights and help reduce biased decisions. A diverse panel brings different viewpoints to the table, helping to identify blind spots and ensure that candidates are evaluated more fairly based on their actual qualifications rather than perceived similarity.

Besides expanding the perspectives of the interviewers, a diversified panel gives a feeling of fit and belongingness to a candidate who comes from underrepresented groups. It sends a strong message of an organization being open and inclusive toward several backgrounds, thus uplifting candidates' confidence and interest during an interview process.

Such would include making the hiring practices inclusive: ensuring that interview panels are representative, the best talent is sought out, and consideration of outcomes is equitably given-a workplace representative of the diverse society at large.

- **Unstructured Interviews**

Casual, unstructured interviews have the potential to greatly increase the risk of biases in hiring decisions. Without a structured format, interviewers are more apt to allow subjective impressions rather than objective criteria to guide their evaluations. This often gives the upper hand to candidates similar in their background, interests, or communication style to that of the interviewer-so-called "similarity bias."

Unstructured interviews can also let unconscious biases, such as assumptions about the capabilities of candidates based on their gender, ethnicity, age, or educational background, pass through. For example, interviewers might make subconscious preferences for outgoing candidates, supposing that outgoingness translates into leadership qualities, while passing over quiet, more introverted candidates who may do exceptionally well in analytical or creative thinking.

Further, unstructured interviews could lead to variation in the criteria on which the evaluation of the candidates is made, as sometimes quite different questions may be put to different candidates or their cases could be matched against different standards. Herein, unfairness is increased and along with that come tough choices that are comparative, yet arbitrary and not merit-based.

The issues identified above could be minimized by the organization through the adoption of structured interviews, where the same procedures are followed for all candidates. This will include a set of predeveloped questions based on the skills, qualifications, and responsibilities required for the job. Structured interviews ensure that each candidate is assessed on the same criteria, reducing the influence of subjective judgments.

Other effective bias minimizers involve the use of scoring rubrics in scoring responses, as these make for clear, objective guidelines of what constitutes performance. Also, multiple interviewers of dissimilar perspectives will help to even out individual biases and come up with more balanced judgments.

A move away from casual, unstructured interviews using a more disciplined and objective approach is critical for making sure the organization picks up people on merit, and not through unconscious bias. Not only does it ensure a fair selection, but also contributes toward developing a diversified and inclusive workplace.

What You Can Do:

- Ensure that your interview panel includes individuals from diverse backgrounds.
- Use standardized questions and scoring rubrics to create a consistent evaluation framework.

Cultural Fit vs. Skill Set

- **What It Really Means**

The idea of hiring for "cultural fit" may be well-intentioned, but all too often it devolves into a system of favoring candidates that closely align with the personalities, interests, and behaviors of current team members. This is often done based on subjective criteria-such as how well the candidate will "fit in" within the current team dynamic-rather than considering if they can bring unique perspective, problem-solving, or innovation.

In prioritizing cultural fit, organizations risk reinforcing unconscious bias toward homogeneity. This could manifest in interviewers subconsciously liking those who went to similar schools, enjoy similar hobbies, or adopt similar communication styles. It is this tendency that automatically shuts out underrepresented populations, who may not conform to the mold of the current culture but had the skill and ideas needed to excel in the job. Over time, hiring out for cultural fit can make a workforce less diverse in their thoughts, experiences, and perspectives, which dampens creativity and innovation.

Besides, this emphasis on cultural fit can be alienating for candidates whose difference in cultural background, work styles, or approaches to challenges could have been assets that benefited the team. Out they go, simply because they do not fit, even though they might be bringing in new ideas and ways that could advance an organization.

The more inclusive hiring for "cultural contribution" does the opposite. It starts to think about how candidates can add to and develop your culture and goals through their experiences, skills, and perspectives. Instead of asking "Will this person fit in?", one is asking questions such as: "How can this person add value to our team?" and "What new perspectives might they bring to our organization?

To implement this, organizations could define their core values and ensure the interview questions are based around these, rather than being subjective to personal preference. Ensuring diverse interview panels and using structured criteria for reviewing candidates can also help make the process less biased and give a greater focus on potential contribution.

Moving away from hiring to fit the culture and embracing cultural contribution is how an organization can be made more dynamic, innovative, and inclusive-actually valuing diversity as a key driver of success.

- **Missed Opportunities**

It inadvertently closes the door on candidates who can bring in perspectives, ideas, and experiences that may be very critical in fostering innovation and driving organizational growth. By making hiring practices too inclined toward conformity rather than diversity, teams become echo chambers where similar ideas are circulated in circles, leaving very little room for fresh and disrupting thinking.

Innovation prospers on the heels of diverse perspectives that question the status quo, catalyze creative problem-solving, and inspire new approaches. Individuals from other cultural backgrounds, educational experiences, or professional trajectories bring insights that often elude the current crop of employees. By filtering out such candidates, companies forfeit chances to expand their thinking and move with changing market demands.

For instance, a group of people with similar mindsets may agree on a course of action without considering what it could mean in a larger perspective or if there are other options. Somebody from a different background can bring another perspective or predict problems others cannot. These can prevent expensive mistakes, reveal unseen opportunities, and give the organization more vitality.

Overreliance on the cultural fit factor creates a setting where employees are pressured into being like everybody else, not being themselves. This makes people less creative and ultimately less engaged, since the employee might be afraid of sharing some unconventional ideas for not fitting in with the "fit" expectations. On the other hand, embracing diverse perspectives fosters psychological safety, encouraging team members to share innovative ideas and collaborate even more effectively.

To avoid the cultural fit trap, organizations should focus on hiring for skill complementarity and cultural contribution. This means actively seeking out people who will challenge current practices constructively and bring new ways of thinking, and creating an environment where different contributions are not only valued but actively invited and celebrated.

The outcome would be teams better equipped to manage complex challenges and seize new opportunities through innovative, resilient, and adaptive means; this would be achieved by shifting the focus from cultural fit toward the value of diverse perspectives.

What You Can Do:

- Shift the focus from "fit" to "culture add," which emphasizes how a candidate can enhance and diversify the existing workplace culture.
- Train hiring managers to recognize and counteract their biases during decision-making.

Additional Steps to Combat Bias in Recruitment and Hiring

- **Diverse Talent Pools:** Partner with organizations that specialize in underrepresented talent, such as women in tech or veterans reentering the workforce.

- **Inclusive Onboarding Practices:** Ensure your onboarding process supports and welcomes new hires, reinforcing a sense of belonging from day one.

- **Continuous Feedback:** Regularly solicit feedback from candidates about their hiring experience to identify areas for improvement.

- By taking proactive steps to minimize bias, organizations can ensure that recruitment and hiring processes are equitable, inclusive, and reflective of the diverse world in which we live.

Engaging Tip:

Try implementing structured interviews and using software tools that mask personal details like names or photos during the initial screening process.

Decision-Making and Leadership

Bias in decision-making can profoundly shape the workplace, affecting who gets hired, promoted, or even heard in discussions. When unchecked, these biases can perpetuate inequities and stifle innovation. Recognizing and addressing these biases is crucial for fostering fairness and effectiveness in leadership.

Common Biases in Decision-Making

1. **Confirmation Bias**

    - **What It Is:** The tendency to seek or prioritize information that supports pre-existing beliefs while ignoring contradictory evidence.

    - **Impact:** Leaders might overlook new ideas or fail to address critical risks because they are focused on validating their initial assumptions.

    - **Example:** A manager assumes a particular team member is unmotivated and interprets their quiet demeanor in meetings as disinterested, overlooking their contributions in written reports.

2. **What You Can Do:**

    - Implement structured decision-making processes that require leaders to consider opposing views or evidence.

    - Encourage a culture of constructive feedback where team members feel safe challenging assumptions.

3. **Affinity Bias**
    - **What It Is:** Favoring individuals who share similar backgrounds, experiences, or interests.
    - **Impact:** Opportunities for advancement may disproportionately go to people who "fit in" rather than those who bring unique perspectives or skills.
    - **Example:** A senior executive may repeatedly mentor and promote employees who share their alma mater, sidelining equally talented individuals.

4. **What You Can Do:**
    - Use objective criteria when evaluating candidates for promotions or new roles.
    - Create formal mentorship programs to ensure equitable access to development opportunities.

5. **Halo Effect**
    - **What It Is:** Allowing one positive trait or achievement to overshadow other

aspects of a person's performance or qualifications.

- **Impact:** Decisions may be based on incomplete evaluations, leading to favoritism or overlooking potential red flags.

- **Example:** Promoting someone to a leadership role based solely on their success in an unrelated technical position without assessing their managerial capabilities.

6. **What You Can Do:**

    - Develop comprehensive evaluation frameworks that assess multiple aspects of performance, including skills, collaboration, and leadership potential.

    - Separate individual traits from overall assessments by using blind scoring systems during evaluations.

Other Biases That May Arise in Leadership

- **Groupthink:** Teams may avoid conflict and align with the perceived consensus, leading to poor decision-making.

- **Recency Bias:** Overemphasizing the most recent events or performances rather than considering a holistic view.

- **Gender and Racial Bias:** Implicit stereotypes can lead to unequal opportunities or recognition for employees from underrepresented groups.

Practical Steps to Address Bias in Leadership Decisions

1. **Data-Driven Decision-Making**
   - Use performance metrics, surveys, and analytics to inform decisions rather than relying solely on subjective judgment.

2. **Diversify Leadership Teams**
   - Encourage diverse representation at all levels of leadership to reduce the influence of homogeneous perspectives.

3. **Regular Bias Training**
    - Conduct workshops to help leaders identify and mitigate their unconscious biases with real-world examples and role-playing scenarios.

4. **Inclusive Decision-Making Practices**
    - Rotate decision-making responsibilities to ensure that all voices are heard and considered.
    - Create forums for anonymous input to give space for alternative ideas without fear of judgment.

Engaging Tip:

Self-Reflection Exercises: Encourage leaders to ask themselves these questions before making decisions:

- Am I relying on assumptions or stereotypes?
- Have I sought input from individuals with different perspectives?
- Does my decision align with the organization's commitment to equity and diversity?

By embedding these practices into decision-making frameworks, organizations can reduce bias, enhance leadership accountability, and cultivate a workplace where talent and effort are the true determinants of success.

Team Dynamics and Interpersonal Relationships

Bias in Team Settings

Biases in team settings can erode trust, collaboration, and productivity, creating an environment where not all members feel valued or included. Recognizing and addressing these biases is essential for fostering strong, equitable teams. Here's how biases might show up and ways to address them effectively.

Microaggressions

Microaggressions are everyday comments or actions—intentional or unintentional—that convey prejudiced assumptions or stereotypes. Examples include:

- **Backhanded Compliments:** Saying, "You're so articulate for someone from [a particular background]," reinforces harmful stereotypes.

- **Tokenism:** Highlighting someone's race, gender, or other identity as their defining trait can make them feel singled out rather than valued for their skills.

- **Assumptive Language:** Phrases like "You wouldn't understand this sports analogy" based on someone's gender can exclude individuals.

What You Can Do:

- Create anonymous reporting channels where team members can share experiences without fear of retaliation.

- Provide training on recognizing and addressing microaggressions.

Uneven Work Distribution

Biases can lead to uneven workloads, with certain employees being overburdened while others are overlooked. This often stems from assumptions like:

- **Competence Bias:** Assuming that a high-performing individual can handle more tasks, leading to burnout.

- **Perceived Weakness:** Assuming that newer or quieter employees cannot handle challenging assignments, which limits their growth opportunities.

What You Can Do:

- Use project management tools to track task assignments and ensure equitable distribution of work.

- Encourage managers to regularly check in with team members to assess workload and provide support where needed.

Exclusionary Behavior

Bias can lead to some team members feeling excluded from informal networks, critical discussions, or even social gatherings. Examples include:

- **Office Cliques:** Groups that form based on shared backgrounds, interests, or tenure can isolate others.

- **Unconscious Gatekeeping:** Excluding individuals from decision-making conversations or high-visibility projects due to assumptions about their capabilities.

What You Can Do:

- Implement inclusive meeting practices, such as rotating facilitators and actively inviting input from all team members.

- Foster a culture of mentorship where senior team members support and guide newer or underrepresented colleagues.

Other Subtle Signs of Bias

- **Stereotyping Roles:** Assuming certain team members are better suited for specific tasks based on their gender, race, or other identity.

- **Communication Bias:** Listening more attentively to some individuals over others, often based on perceived authority or charisma.

- **Recognition Gaps:** Overlooking contributions from underrepresented team members while frequently acknowledging others.

Engaging Tips for Tackling Bias in Teams

- **Encourage Open Conversations:** Create a safe space for team members to voice concerns about bias. Active listening and mutual respect are key.

- **Host Inclusivity Workshops:** Provide practical, interactive training to help team members recognize and challenge their own biases.

- **Build Cross-Functional Teams:** Assigning diverse team members to projects encourages collaboration and fosters understanding across different perspectives.

- **Celebrate Individual Contributions:** Highlight the unique strengths and achievements of each team member to reinforce their value to the group.

Final Thoughts:

Recognizing bias is the first step toward building an equitable workplace. Organizations should commit to regular process reviews, invest in employee education, and encourage open dialogue. A workplace free from bias is not only fairer but also more innovative and productive.

THE ROLE OF DATA IN ADDRESSING BIAS

Data plays a pivotal role in identifying and addressing biases, especially when it comes to promoting fairness, equity, and inclusion. By leveraging the right tools and analyzing trends, organizations can make informed decisions to create more equitable environments. Let's break it down:

Tools and Metrics to Assess Bias

Think of tools as the magnifying glass that allows you to closely examine hidden patterns of bias. Whether it's in hiring practices, promotional opportunities, or everyday decision-making, these tools provide the clarity needed to uncover blind spots. Here are some standard tools and metrics:

1. **Diversity Dashboards**

Diversity dashboards are a critical tool in every organization's equity and inclusion work. The dashboard gives them the actual country's demographic makeup of their teams in real-time data, giving them the ongoing pulse of workplace diversity. This lets them track, across different levels in organizations, various metrics including gender, ethnicity, and age amongst others. These dashboards highlight the inequalities that may take place so that the leadership could make concrete decisions rather than just assumption-based decisions.

For example, it could be the gender or ethnic composition in leadership versus the rest of the workforce. If the talent pool is pretty diverse at the lower levels and a small group dominates at the very top, such data are a signal toward targeted interventions. These insights provide organizations with the ability to evaluate the impact of hiring, promotion, and retention strategies on stated goals regarding inclusivity.

Besides serving identification purposes, diversity dashboards create accountability. With crystal-clear line-of-sight views to progress-or lack of it-teams and leaders are much more motivated to actually do something about inequalities and change the situation. Furthermore, such tools are inclined to make data more accessible for all people at an organization and hence build transparency, forcing everyone to take responsibility collectively for inclusivity.

Diversity dashboards ultimately take raw data and make it into actionable insights, equipping the organization with what it needs to create a workplace where everyone has an equal opportunity to thrive.

2. AI-Powered Audits

Artificial Intelligence has become an important ally in the process of pointing out and mitigating these biases, especially in language used within organizations. Job descriptions and performance evaluations, though key elements of professional processes, tend to inadvertently mirror subtle biases that discourage certain groups from applying or thriving at a workplace. AI is one of the transformational solutions for such challenges.

Through sophisticated algorithms, AI tools analyze texts for the use of language that may unconsciously exclude or disadvantage certain groups. Examples include the use of terms like "rockstar" or "ninja" in job postings, which may be attractive to one demographic group but a turn-off to others. Other examples involve adjectives such as "aggressive" or "domineering" in performance reviews, perhaps meting out undeserved penalties for those demonstrating another, equally successful style of leadership.

Innovative platforms like Textio and Gender Decoder stand guard for inclusive communication. These tools rate and underline the bad language, suggesting alternatives that can strike a chord with the audience. Rather than flagging issues, they provide actionable recommendations to make sure job postings and internal evaluations foster a sense of belonging. When organizations integrate such tools, they reduce not only the risk of perpetuating biases but also enhance their ability to attract diverse talent and create an equitable workplace culture.

In other words, AI does more than just help organizations communicate more inclusively; it reshapes how they think of and value language, turning it into a conduit for opportunity and equity.

3. **Employee Feedback Surveys**

It creates avenues through which employees can share experiences openly and safely; this is really important for making a truly inclusive workplace. Collecting anonymous feedback serves as a strong mechanism for this. Workers, knowing they can safely voice their concerns without retaliation, are more likely to provide candid insights into their experiences with unfair treatment, bias, or system-wide challenges within an organization. This approach tends to reveal masked problems and gives employees a hint that their voices are vital, thereby gaining trust and building confidence in the leadership.

Anonymous feedback also yields data that can be transformed into actionable insights. For example, metrics such as an inclusivity score offer a tangible way to measure how welcomed, valued, and supported employees feel in their roles. Such metrics go beyond surface-level representation, diving into the quality of the employee experience. Inclusion scores, when tracked over time, help highlight progress or identify persistent gaps, which enables organizations to fine-tune their diversity and inclusion strategies.

Anonymous feedback and inclusivity metrics, when combined, will allow an organization to take a complete look at its culture and proactively make adjustments where needed. This would be a work environment where every individual feels empowered, respected, and genuinely included.

4. **Performance Metrics Analysis**

Performance review analytics can help organizations identify patterns that might indicate a difference in how groups are being evaluated. This includes the language, ratings, and overall feedback given to different demographics based on gender, ethnicity, or age. For example, it may show that some groups consistently get less favorable feedback despite similar outcomes.

These discrepancies, when identified, will help the organization identify where unconscious bias may influence evaluations. This will also make sure that performance reviews truly reflect an individual's merit, contributions, and potential rather than being influenced by stereotypes or preconceived notions. The ultimate goal is to create a more objective and equitable evaluation process, fostering a workplace where all employees feel recognized and valued for their genuine achievements.

These analytics will give an organization more reasons and ways to work toward committing to improve the review process, thereby engendering equity, trust, and ultimately motivating the workforce to produce productivity and a great atmosphere.

With these tools, data isn't just numbers on a screen; it's a mirror reflecting how fair and inclusive an organization truly is.

Analyzing Trends in Representation and Opportunity

Data doesn't just show where biases exist—it helps paint the bigger picture of how they evolve. This is crucial for creating long-term solutions. Let's explore two key areas:

1. **Representation Trends**

    - **What to Track:** Representation metrics focus on the demographic makeup of employees across levels—entry, middle management, and leadership.

    - **Why It Matters:** If trends show little progress in promoting underrepresented groups to leadership, this signals systemic barriers that need to be addressed.

- **Example:** A tech company notices its engineering team remains 90% male despite inclusive hiring efforts. This could prompt a deeper analysis of recruitment practices and workplace culture.

2. **Opportunity Trends**

    - **What to Track:** Opportunity metrics measure who is getting access to promotions, raises, training, and mentorship.

    - **Why It Matters:** Bias often manifests in unequal opportunities, even when representation seems balanced.

    - **Example:** If data reveals that women in a company receive fewer promotions than their male counterparts despite similar performance ratings, it indicates a need for more equitable advancement processes.

Data-driven insights like these help organizations move beyond vague assumptions to actionable strategies. By focusing on both representation and opportunities, companies can better align their practices with their commitment to diversity and inclusion.

THE POWER OF HUMANIZING DATA

While numbers tell an important story, it's essential to remember that behind every data point is a real person with unique experiences. Humanizing the data ensures that decisions aren't just about checking boxes but about improving lives.

Humanizing data means to transform abstract numbers into meaningful stories that strike a chord in the hearts of people. Every number has a story, a lived experience that provides insight into what representation, inclusion, and opportunity look like. By sharing these stories, cold statistics can be turned into powerful calls to action that evoke empathy and create meaningful change. For example, a testimonial from an employee who shares how mentorship programs helped them to get over some kind of career obstacle and to grow will be able to showcase organizational initiatives in real-world settings. Stories like these don't just confirm the value of equity-related practices; they motivate leaders to invest even more in such programs that are really helping people.

To truly make data accessible and appealing, visualization is key. Infographics, charts, and visual dashboards present complex data in ways more digestible by anyone within an organization. A well-designed infographic of improvements in diversity or representation overtime could very well be far more compelling than an extensive report full of tiny text. It invites stakeholders into the information to create a shared view of where the organization currently resides and in what direction it needs to head.

Equally important will be the engagement of employees on the path of understanding and acting from insight contained within the data. When the workforce is invited to discuss what the data says, it creates shared ownership. Such discussions bring out valuable insights that numbers themselves may not catch-for example, some cultural nuances or workplace dynamics affecting trends. Collaborative sessions, where employees and leadership brainstorm actionable solutions based on data findings, create transparency and build trust. They make data analysis a team sport, so to speak, in which everyone feels empowered to make meaningful changes.

By weaving storytelling, visual tools, and collaborative engagement into the process, organizations can ensure that data will be alive and breathing in their culture-to point out challenges while inspiring collective action toward equity and inclusion.

Data is a powerful ally in the fight against bias. By using tools to assess bias and analyze trends in representation and opportunity, organizations can take meaningful steps toward building a more inclusive and equitable workplace. However, it's not just about crunching numbers—it's about understanding the people those numbers represent. When data is used thoughtfully, it becomes the bridge that connects intentions with impactful action.

PERSONAL REFLECTION

Understanding ourselves deeply is a crucial step toward personal growth, especially when it comes to uncovering our biases. Our biases, both conscious and unconscious, shape how we perceive the world and interact with others. Here, we'll explore strategies to uncover these biases and tools to help us identify and reflect on them.

Strategies for Individuals to Uncover Their Own Biases

- **Self-Reflection Journaling**

Perhaps one of the most powerful ways to discover your biases is through reflective practice. The moment you take the time to explore your thoughts, experiences, and interactions, you begin to create an opportunity to realize the underlying set of beliefs and assumptions that might shape your perceptions. In this respect, journaling becomes a useful tool. You begin to know your own mind and what patterns may influence your behavior as you write down your thoughts.

Questions would be good to ask of oneself at this stage. *For example, "What assumptions about others do I make?" or "How different are my reactions when relating with people coming from other walks of life?"* These prompt you for deeper inquiry when biases perhaps might arise. Reflective moments when discomfort or judgment are felt give insight again, where assumptions steer one's conduct.

In this process, you start to observe repeating themes or tendencies; how perhaps sets of people lead to particular responses. Further, the recognition of such patterns will help you discover hidden prejudices and how they might affect your thoughts and actions. The more aware you get, the easier it is to counteract and change.

Self-awareness cultivates more awareness that then enables you to navigate these situations with more empathy and intentionality. This process promotes not only the recognition of biases over time but deeper understanding of others to form the foundation for far more inclusive and meaningful contact.

- **Feedback from Others**

Another effective method of finding the hidden biases is to ask feedback from friends, family members, or colleagues. They might see something that we can't ourselves. It may be done by asking them questions so that certain behaviors or attitudes controlled by unconscious biases will be highlighted.

For instance, one may ask if he feels there is a pattern in the way one acts or reacts with groups of people, or if he doesn't think that one's view reflects biases one is not aware of. These questions give insight into one's interactions and make observations that may bring up blind spots within their thinking.

This is such a potent approach because people often will notice things about us that we do not even realize in our own right. Over time, biases can get deeply inculcated, and since they operate at an unconscious level, it becomes easy not to notice how they guide our actions, beliefs, or judgments. Opening yourself up to feedback is offering a chance at new insights you might never otherwise have.

The feedback you receive can also be used to understand how biases manifest in real-life interactions. For example, your friend may tell you that you always assume certain traits in people of other cultural backgrounds, while your colleague may notice how you act differently in diverse settings. This is a critical self-awareness which helps you understand where to grow.

In the end, seeking feedback not only raises your awareness of biases but also creates openness and humility to engage others in a more thoughtful and empathetic way.

- **Exposure to Different Perspectives**

Most bias comes from being ignorant of the diversity around and, therefore, people will often assume things about other people different from themselves. This calls for exposure to new experiences, conversations, and relationships with people from other backgrounds, cultures, and beliefs. Interaction with various individuals will help in further challenging the existing beliefs, break down stereotypes, and deepening one's understanding of the world.

This may also be effectively done through the reading of books from varied perspectives, workshops on understanding other cultures, or from different thinking, and seeing yourself learn how to broaden perspectives without biased opinions. These changes will come into the realm of view by asking several personal questions such as how do my experiences differ from those around me?

Realizing that not everyone lives life in the same manner, and that cultural background, upbringing, and individual experiences make a difference, opens your eyes to realize how your own view can be narrow or incomplete.

What assumptions do I make that are based on limited knowledge?

Bias is often based on generalization or superficial interpretation of information. Being able to reflect on these assumptions enables you to question their origins and understand the deeper context that constitutes other people's lives.

By challenging your assumptions and trying to understand different perspectives, you open yourself up to a broader, richer view of the world. This effort not only enhances empathy but also encourages more inclusive and meaningful interactions with people from all walks of life.

Mindfulness and Awareness Practices

Mindfulness significantly helps in developing self-awareness by making us more aware of our thoughts and reactions. When one stays present in a conversation, reflecting upon what he says, he develops a deeper realization of how his automatic responses or assumptions may affect the interaction. These things usually happen unconsciously, which is how biases can slip into our actions and go unnoticed.

Consider the example of someone whose opinion is different from yours. Instead of immediately degrading or going on the defense, mindfulness brings you to stay present, observing emotional and cognitive responses. Ask yourself:

Why do I feel uneasy or dismissive?

What assumptions am I making that might be causing this discomfort?

This, in turn, helps you to recognize those moments when biases are at play in your thinking or actions. It leaves room for a pause, some reflection, and challenging of these assumptions so that you can respond with more empathy and openness.

With time, mindfulness decreases the automaticity of biased responses and replaces it with reflective and inclusive interactions. The more you are aware of how you respond to views that differ from yours, the more you can begin to shift your understanding and connect on a deeper level with others.

Exercises and Self-Assessment Tools

- **Implicit Association Tests (IAT)**

Researchers develop Implicit Association Tests as web tools that can serve to help uncover the biases at our subconscious levels, which we may not fully realize. These tests work by measuring the speed and ease with which you associate certain words, images, or concepts with specific groups of people. The idea is that quicker, automatic associations often reflect underlying biases that influence our thoughts and behaviors without us realizing it.

Indeed, the taking of an IAT may be rather illuminating: deep-seated patterns of bias yet blind to conscious awareness become apparent. You might just find yourself out to have unconsciously linked groups with certain characteristics or traits. That is the surprising thing about this: these biases run opposite of even our conscious beliefs or ideals.

Completing an IAT allows immense insight into one's thought process and can bring to the forefront biases of which one was not even aware. Websites such as the Implicit Bias Test at Harvard (implicit.harvard.edu) make the process very smooth and accessible in completing online. These tests are about the different biases based on race, gender, age, or cultural background.

These tests can indeed yield quite revealing results, putting into perspective areas where your biases might lead your thoughts and interactions. More importantly, they create avenues for reflection and growth: to question these automatic links and to be more thoughtful in your actions and choices. Taking the test is a crucial step toward greater self-awareness and a more inclusive perspective.

- **Bias Diaries**

A bias diary is kept similar to a self-reflection journal, but it holds a particular record of observations of instances where one noticed biased thoughts, feelings, or actions. The core difference is that while general introspection is encouraged with any other form of journaling, a bias diary specifically zeroes in on when the bias manifests, allowing more structure to the process of increasing self-awareness.

Each time you catch a biased thought or reaction, notice the context: where you were, who was involved, and what exactly happened. Reflecting on these details may help you identify situations and triggers that could lead to biases. You may notice that there are groups of people around whom you tend to feel uncomfortable or judged, or maybe you notice that because of preconceived beliefs or assumptions, you act differently. Recording these events helps to bring clarity to the underlying biases influencing your behavior.

The bias diary helps you notice patterns and trends if you go through it regularly. You may notice, over time, that there are recurring themes or particular situations that tend to make you have biased thoughts. By tracking these instances, you can begin to understand the root causes of your biases and how they show up in different aspects of your life, whether in relationships, workplace interactions, or even daily encounters.

This process fosters not only the surfacing of these hidden biases but also develops an intentional reflection process whereby such patterns, once identified, can be challenged and reshaped into more aware, inclusive ways of relating with others.

- **Cultural Experience Mapping**

The mapping of those who have crossed your path or with whom you've interacted will give you a profound understanding of your worldviews: how it is and was formed. Such a map allows the facilitator to trace such influences-whether they be through people they have interacted with, the cultural setting in which they have existed, or through life-changing experiences that seem to form them. This map gives insight into where one's exposure has been limited or narrow, which may have been the cause of bias.

Jot down moments, relationships, or environments that you feel have defined your understanding of the world. Ask yourself: Who are the most influential people in my life? What cultures, backgrounds, or traditions have I been around? Are there groups or perspectives I haven't deeply engaged with?

But most people, as they go exploring their map, find missing pieces—places where, in your life, interactions have been limited to perhaps a few people, maybe a few cultures, few opinions. Perhaps your upbringing and environment led you to the same community or belief structure but did not allow varied perspectives to enter into or enrich your life. Such gaps are where biases have a tendency to form.

These are often filled by making conscious efforts to reach out for cultures, backgrounds, and perspectives that one is not accustomed to. It can be reading books from authors of other cultures, attending seminars or workshops about diversity, or developing relationships with individuals from backgrounds unfamiliar to one's own. This conscious push will allow you to widen your experiences, thus changing preconceived ideas into a deeper understanding of life.

You do this by showing empathy, making fewer assumptions, and having a far richer, more inclusive outlook. The investigation of these blind spots not only serves to reveal prejudices but also helps you further develop your capacity for meaningful connections to others, contributing toward openness and compassion in the world.

- **Mindful Listening Practice**

Now, the next time, pay more attention to your conversations-particularly those where you might feel that your beliefs or assumptions are being challenged. Discomfort or disagreement serves as a goldmine for growth. You will notice in these conversations with people holding different views from yours that it is actually curiosity and openness that are expected of you rather than suddenly being defensive or shut down. Try to understand where this other person is coming from without interrupting or judging.

This is where active listening plays a major role, paying attention to what the other person says, asking for an explanation of some unclear points, and making sure you got their meaning across. Open-ended questions help make a discussion broader and give an opportunity to turn to another direction in conversation easily. For example, instead of asking a closed question like "Do you agree with me?

Ask something like, "Can you tell me more about your perspective on this?" or "What led you to that conclusion?" In so doing, it means you are developing a curiosity interest in learning and trying to understand others' views-a reason that will make a person develop empathy and eliminate bias when making decisions. This helps you in building further knowledge, challenging your assumptions, and thereby forming better, inclusive relationships.

Uncovering biases is a continuous journey that requires self-awareness, reflection, and openness to change. By using self-assessment tools, engaging in thoughtful exercises, and embracing different perspectives, we can move toward a more inclusive and understanding mindset. The more aware we become, the more we can create authentic connections and foster empathy in our interactions with others.

PART III: ADDRESSING AND REDUCING BIAS

CREATING AN INCLUSIVE CULTURE

The Importance of Psychological Safety

Psychological safety is a foundational element in fostering an inclusive culture. It refers to the feeling of being safe to express thoughts, ideas, and concerns without fear of negative consequences like judgment, ridicule, or punishment. When employees feel psychologically safe, they are more likely to contribute openly, collaborate effectively, and feel a sense of belonging.

Why Psychological Safety Matters

Psychological safety is central to achieving a successful and diverse workplace where individuals can bring their whole self to work. The basic underlying concept in psychological safety entails a setting whereby one is allowed to comfortably share his or her mind, ideas, and thoughts without fear of judgment, rejection, or reprisal. In psychologically safe settings, people are most likely to offer their insight and ideas and voice their concerns, taking creative risks for better solving and innovation of problems.

One of the key benefits that come with psychological safety is open communication. If people feel safe, they can say what is uniquely on their minds, ask questions, and admit mistakes without any fear of judgment. This openness leads to a culture of learning and collaboration, where diverse ideas are put forward and valued. Hence, teams can approach challenges with fresh perspectives-leading to more innovative solutions and better decision-making.

It will also help in building trust and respect within teams: once employees feel safe to express themselves, that sets up the bedrock of trust. Trust is important for healthy relationships, reducing misunderstandings, and creating a sense of connection between colleagues. This will help in reducing conflicts and building an atmosphere where respect thrives. People will invest more in their work when they feel that their contributions are valued, and this leads to better teamwork and a feeling of mutual support.

Psychological safety has a direct effect on engagement and productivity: When people realize that they will not be penalized for their ideas or mistakes, they are most likely to take ownership of their work and contribute actively. Because when employees are confident that everything is secure around them, they pour their best talents into whatever they are working on; they are unafraid of taking calculated risks. And when people are engaged yet secure, they're motivated, with security at their work empowering them to challenge the status quo without an element of fear. In other words, psychological safety makes the employees become interested in, and concerned for, the general success of the organization, rather than just committing to their immediate jobs.

Ultimately, creating a culture of psychological safety isn't about reducing fear but rather about unleashing potential, creating collaboration, and empowering people to thrive. When employees can be themselves without fear, they contribute with more authenticity, build stronger relationships, and become more motivated in pursuit of personal and organizational goals alike.

1. **Benefits of Psychological Safety in the Workplace**

    - **Improved Collaboration and Innovation**: Teams that feel safe to share diverse ideas tend to innovate and solve problems more effectively.

    - **Reduced Workplace Bias**: Employees who feel safe are more likely to recognize and challenge biases, leading to a more equitable work environment.

    - **Increased Well-being**: Psychological safety contributes to overall employee well-being, reducing stress and enhancing job satisfaction.

Strategies for Promoting Equity

Creating an inclusive culture requires intentional efforts to promote equity—ensuring fairness and access to opportunities for all employees, regardless of their background.

1. **Diversify Hiring and Promotion Practices**

Inclusive hiring is a major tool to reduce unconscious bias in hiring. Identifying information like the applicant's name, gender, and ethnicity needs to be removed from their resume so that organizations have an objective method of selection. It will help keep the concentration on skills, qualification, and experience rather than subjective assumptions on demographic factors. Blind hiring is one way to provide a platform where all applicants stand an equal chance of being considered, solely on merit.

Apart from bias being taken away from the process of hiring, one must undertake comprehensive training in biases for the hiring manager/teams. These training help them understand and further create awareness regarding unconscious bias, assumptions, or stereotypes that a person may hold about others without him/her knowing about it. Training hiring teams on how biases can impact decision-making empowers them to acknowledge and overcome those biases. Real-life scenarios, handy tools, and advice on how to avoid unintentional favor or discriminatory behavior are commonly covered in training sessions.

It's not just a matter of reducing bias; it's about creating a culture that considers diversity and inclusion at every step of the recruitment and selection process.

Other major strategies that can ensure or help promote equity within workplaces are equal opportunities. Promoting access to training, mentorship, career advancement programs, and promotional opportunities will go a long way in making the setting inclusive for all employees regardless of their background. Providing all with equal opportunities to improve their skill sets, growing within a career path of interest, and contributing constructively toward organizational goals is greatly facilitated. This further helps in breaking down systemic barriers that have always obstructed certain groups of people from pursuing opportunities. The organization can unleash the capabilities of all its employees to make sure it has a more diverse and successful workforce by fostering a culture of fairness and support.

2. **Foster Inclusive Leadership**

Leaders are influential in setting cultures within an inclusive workplace environment. They can be the cause of much good since leading through role modeling leads to leading through inclusive behaviors: promoting respect, driving equity, and reducing biases. Indeed, they could set a benchmark within any organization, showing fairness and respect for all-something that will be quite useful if employees find themselves wanting to be similar, making it a welcoming atmosphere for one and all.

Besides role modeling, accountability is very important. There is a need for an organization to set clear expectations from their leaders in bringing about an inclusive workplace. Accountability will make the leaders walk the talk, and hence, the establishment of measurable goals on issues of DEI, and have leaders assessed from time to time regarding performance. Accountability reinforces the role of inclusion and sends messages that fostering a diverse and respectful environment is not only a priority but a responsibility for all across the leadership spectrum.

The third very key element is empowerment: being sure to listen and let your teams have the air, embracing diverse opinions, and encouraging open interaction. The point of promoting equity is to create environments where people of all backgrounds are safe to share thoughts, concerns, and ideas. On a deeper level, gaining insight into challenges and barriers that employees are experiencing lets leaders listen to their teams and then make more informed decisions in a manner that supports inclusion, removing systemic obstacles. Empower the employees to contribute to decision-making itself, which means diverse voices are not only being heard but also integrated into the culture, making any outcome meaningful and inclusive.

3. Create Supportive Policies and Practices

Flexible Work Arrangements

Flexibility in work arrangements is important for equity in the workplace because they value and support diverse needs of all employees, whether it be working from home, adjusting hours to accommodate personal commitments, or flexible scheduling; such work arrangements allow employees to balance their professional responsibilities with caregiving, personal health needs, or other circumstances. By allowing choices that give more leeway to workers as relates to work schedules, the employers prove that they have employees' welfare at heart. Flexibility in work often causes the feeling of less stress and a higher productivity level for many employees, who feel so well with their job placements since their individual life circumstances are considered. The feeling created is one of trust, respect, and belonging; thus, the workplace becomes equitable and flexible.

Inclusive Benefits

Inclusive benefits are fundamental to the equitably designed workplace. Making sure healthcare, parental leave, and professional development opportunities are available to all workers, regardless of their backgrounds, enhances fairness and promotes wellbeing. For instance, full healthcare coverage that covers an array of needs-such as mental health care, family planning, or accommodations for disabilities-means that employees feel supported in their health journeys. It is also crucial that parental leave policies include, but are not limited to, the statutory minimum, while offering opportunities for both primary and secondary caregivers. Policies guaranteeing equal access to professional development opportunities-through training programs, mentorship, or career advancement-are also essential for all employees. When designed to be inclusive, benefits not only help retain top talent but also add to the feeling of fairness and belonging within the organization.

Employee Resource Groups (ERGs)

ERGs reckon allowing a safe space for the underrepresented to, therefore, foster inclusiveness. These groups are a source of community within an organization for employees to relate, share experiences, and promote interests. ERGs create an avenue where people come together, ensuring that all diverse views of the people get represented and heard. They serve as active networks for visibility, support, and development in order to decrease feelings of isolation and promote further understanding. ERGs stimulate open discussion on issues of bias, discrimination, and inequality, making it easier to deal with within organizations. Activities such as workshops, mentorship programs, and advocacy activities by ERGs build an enabling environment in the workplace culture with regard to the well-being of each individual employee. Driving change by empowering underrepresented groups through the fostering of community, ERGs are how the organization ensures real growth toward true inclusion.

4. Encourage Open Dialogue and Feedback

The facilitation of safe spaces for conversation goes a long way in nurturing an inclusive culture that empowers employees to make their own personal experiences with bias and inequity known. Such safe spaces indeed afford them psychological safety: they are free to say anything without being belittled or even persecuted. From formalized forums of discussion to group or one-on-one talks, such settings would encourage workers to share their concerns, describe the inequalities they may face, and provide good ideas on barriers that exist. A feeling among people that they are heard and heeded could get them to more contribution to solutions at achieving equity and inclusion.

In addition to safe spaces, feedback mechanisms are also essential for gathering information on the presence of bias and how it can be dealt with. The anonymity of the channels through which such responses may be made, by means of surveys or through a suggestion box, allows free and frank responses without any retribution. These mechanisms will expose hidden biases and give substantive support to action. The information gathered in regard to experiences and perceptions of employees helps the organizations in identifying patterns, measuring progress, and pinpointing certain areas that need improvement.

Equity is further enhanced by listening sessions that create avenues for employees to air their views, share personal stories, and offer actionable recommendations. Regularly scheduled sessions run by the leadership or a dedicated team allow employees to speak openly about bias they might have faced and offer a platform for their voices and concerns both as individuals and groups. The discussions are not only crucial in developing deep insight into the specific challenges of the underrepresented groups but also build an atmosphere of empathy and continuous improvement. When employees feel that their concerns are heard and taken seriously, and actions are indeed taken, this builds trust and strengthens momentum toward equity.

5. **Measure and Monitor Progress**

Therefore, data collection is of critical essence in measuring the success of a diversity and inclusion program. The organization will, from tracking key diversity metrics on representation across different levels, the composition of leadership teams, and participation in development programs, obtain useful insights into areas where progress has been made or gaps still remain. Besides that, one should follow up on changes in such metrics, as it would ensure that efforts toward bias reduction actually translate into real improvement. This is a good way to track trends, successes, and areas that may need more attention or adjustment.

Check-ins are important in keeping the momentum going and in making sure the initiative of inclusion remains pointed toward the goals of the organization. These check-ins go beyond simple progress reports; rather, they deal with deeper evaluations of how initiatives are evolving. In these, leaders and teams can assess what's working, gather feedback from employees, and identify barriers that still need to be discussed through open dialogue. This could be done through quarterly reviews, feedback sessions, or broader organizational audits; check-ins provide opportunities to refine policies, adjust practices, and assure continuous improvement in efforts towards inclusion.

Celebrating wins is more than acknowledging milestones; rather, it builds a culture of valuing and amplifying success. By acknowledging individual, team, and organization-wide achievements, it encourages positive behaviors and begets a sense of belonging motivating greater commitments to inclusivity. By publicly demonstrating progress, through events, small acknowledgments, or other celebrations, momentum will build, pride will grow in an organization committed to equity. In that process, celebration becomes integral as it allows companies to make the process of working toward inclusivity sustainable and to understand that every step ahead contributes to a more inclusive workplace.

By prioritizing psychological safety and implementing strategies for promoting equity, organizations can build a workplace where everyone feels valued, respected, and empowered. Reducing bias leads to a more diverse, equitable, and inclusive environment that benefits both employees and the organization as a whole.

STRATEGIES FOR PROMOTING EQUITY

Promoting equity is about ensuring fairness and providing equal opportunities to all individuals, regardless of their background or identity. Here are several key strategies that organizations, communities, and individuals can adopt to promote equity in various settings.

Encourage Diversity and Inclusion

Diversity refers to the presence of various identities, including race, gender, age, ethnicity, socioeconomic background, sexual orientation, and abilities, within a group. It recognizes the value of differences and promotes the representation of individuals from different walks of life. Inclusion, on the other hand, focuses on creating an environment where everyone feels respected, supported, and empowered to contribute fully, regardless of their background. Inclusion ensures that individuals from marginalized groups have a sense of belonging, are treated fairly, and have equal opportunities to thrive.

How to Implement:

- **Recruit from a Variety of Backgrounds**

Ensuring that your recruitment efforts are not limited to a specific demographic is crucial in promoting equity within your organization. Casting a wide net by sourcing candidates from various communities, networks, and institutions opens the door to a more diverse pool of talent. Reaching out to community organizations, universities, and networks that represent underrepresented populations allows you to tap into a rich pool of qualified individuals who may otherwise be overlooked. These organizations often have established relationships with diverse groups, providing valuable insights and connections that can enhance your recruitment efforts. By fostering these partnerships, you not only broaden your candidate pool but also demonstrate a commitment to inclusivity, ensuring that your organization reflects the diverse communities it serves.

- **Create Inclusive Policies and Practices**

To indeed promote fairness, equity, and equal opportunity within an organization, the establishment of clear, intentional policies is essential. These policies serve as the foundation for ensuring that all employees, regardless of their background, have access to the same opportunities for success. For instance, adopting unbiased hiring practices ensures that recruitment decisions are made based solely on qualifications and capabilities rather than biases rooted in factors such as race, gender, or socioeconomic status. Pay equity policies are equally critical, ensuring that individuals are compensated fairly for their contributions without being influenced by discriminatory practices. Flexible work arrangements further support equity by recognizing that employees have varying needs, allowing them to balance their professional responsibilities with personal commitments.

Incorporating diversity and inclusion (D&I) goals into an organization's strategic objectives ensures that these principles are not merely add-ons but are integral to the company's mission and success. D&I goals should be established as key performance indicators (KPIs) to track progress and hold teams accountable. By linking these goals to performance metrics, organizations demonstrate a commitment to creating inclusive environments and ensure that diversity efforts are systematically evaluated and improved upon. When D&I goals are integrated into organizational performance frameworks, they become a fundamental aspect of decision-making, recruitment, retention, and career advancement strategies.

Equally important is the practice of regularly reviewing and updating policies to reflect changing needs and challenges around inclusion. The dynamic nature of work environments, societal norms, and organizational structures means that policies must evolve to remain effective. Continuous assessment of policies ensures they remain relevant, addressing emerging issues such as unconscious bias, evolving workplace dynamics, and new forms of discrimination that may arise. Organizations should actively engage in regular feedback loops—gathering insights from employees, tracking diversity metrics, and revisiting policies to ensure they align with current values and goals. By keeping these policies adaptive and responsive, organizations can foster a more inclusive culture that grows in tandem with societal progress.

Encourage Participation from Marginalized Groups in Decision-Making Processes

Involving diverse voices in leadership, committees, and decision-making processes is essential for promoting equity. When organizations actively seek out and embrace a broad spectrum of perspectives, they benefit from the unique insights and experiences that underrepresented groups bring to the table. These diverse voices help illuminate blind spots, challenge assumptions, and create more inclusive solutions. By integrating people from various backgrounds—whether based on race, gender, age, or socioeconomic status—organizations can ensure that decisions are made with a deeper understanding of the diverse needs of their communities.

One effective way to facilitate this is by creating platforms like advisory councils, task forces, or feedback sessions. These spaces provide marginalized groups with a direct channel to contribute their expertise, ideas, and concerns. Dedicated forums for underrepresented voices ensure that their input is not only heard but also valued, promoting a sense of belonging and agency. These spaces should not be seen as one-off initiatives but rather as integral parts of ongoing efforts to maintain inclusivity and accountability.

It's crucial, however, to avoid tokenism when promoting equity through representation. Tokenism occurs when individuals from marginalized groups are included to fulfill a quota or appear diverse without genuine power or influence. Authentic representation requires more than surface-level participation—it demands meaningful engagement and the opportunity to influence decision-making. Organizations should ensure that diverse voices are not only included but have absolute authority and the ability to shape policies, practices, and outcomes. Accurate equity comes from amplifying the voices of those who have historically been excluded and ensuring that they play a critical role in shaping an inclusive future.

Offer Training and Workshops to Raise Awareness About Biases and Foster a Culture of Inclusion

Providing unconscious bias training is a crucial step in helping employees become more aware of the biases they may hold, which can often influence behavior, hiring practices, and decision-making. These biases, often unconscious, are deeply ingrained and can affect judgments without individuals realizing it. By recognizing these biases, employees can better understand how they might inadvertently favor or exclude certain groups, whether in recruitment, promotions, or daily interactions. Training sessions focused on unconscious bias encourage self-reflection and critical thinking, equipping employees with the tools to challenge these assumptions and make fairer, more objective decisions.

In addition to unconscious bias training, offering workshops on cultural competence, microaggressions, and effective communication in diverse settings can play a vital role in fostering empathy and understanding. Cultural competence workshops help employees gain a deeper awareness of cultural differences, enabling them to navigate cross-cultural interactions more effectively. These sessions emphasize the importance of empathy, respect, and the need to adapt communication styles to ensure everyone feels heard and valued. Microaggressions—subtle, often unintended forms of discrimination—are also explored in these workshops, helping participants identify and address them in both personal and professional settings.

Furthermore, encouraging ongoing dialogue around issues of inclusion, equity, and diversity ensures that these conversations remain active and relevant. Creating spaces for employees to share their experiences, concerns, and ideas helps break down barriers and cultivate a culture of respect and accountability. Through regular discussions, employees are encouraged to reflect on their role in promoting equity and inclusion, fostering a sense of responsibility for creating a more inclusive environment. These conversations can be facilitated through meetings, focus groups, or virtual platforms, providing a safe space for honest dialogue and continuous learning. Ultimately, the goal is to embed a culture of accountability where equity and diversity are prioritized, and all employees feel empowered to contribute to a more inclusive workplace.

Why It Matters:

When organizations and communities wholeheartedly embrace diversity and inclusion, they unlock a multitude of benefits that extend far beyond the surface. At its core, embracing diversity means recognizing and valuing differences—whether in race, gender, age, background, or thought—creating environments where everyone feels welcomed, respected, and empowered. This not only enhances the internal dynamics of organizations but also contributes to broader societal progress.

One of the most significant benefits of embracing diversity is the boost to creativity and innovation. A diverse group brings together a wide array of perspectives, backgrounds, and experiences. When people from different walks of life collaborate, they approach problems with unique lenses, enabling out-of-the-box thinking and fresh ideas that might never emerge from a homogeneous team. This kind of inclusive environment fosters an atmosphere where diverse teams are better equipped to generate innovative solutions, particularly for complex, multifaceted challenges.

Diversity also promotes more effective problem-solving. When teams are composed of individuals with varied experiences and viewpoints, the risk of "groupthink" diminishes. Groupthink occurs when the desire for consensus stifles critical thinking, leading to poor decision-making. By contrast, diverse teams encourage open dialogue and discussions that challenge assumptions, broaden perspectives, and ensure that multiple viewpoints are considered. This leads to better, more informed decisions as team members leverage their collective knowledge and experiences to navigate obstacles creatively.

Beyond creativity and problem-solving, diversity and inclusion contribute to increased employee engagement and retention. When individuals feel valued and respected for who they are, they are more likely to be engaged in their work. Inclusive environments foster a sense of belonging, creating workplaces where employees feel supported, connected, and motivated. This leads to higher job satisfaction, a greater commitment to organizational goals, and, ultimately, lower turnover rates. People want to work in environments where they can thrive, be authentic, and feel they are part of a community that values their contributions.

When organizations implement inclusive hiring practices, a broader talent pool becomes accessible. Diversity in recruitment ensures that talent isn't overlooked due to biases related to race, gender, or socioeconomic status. By seeking out candidates from underrepresented groups, organizations can tap into a wealth of untapped potential. This approach not only helps meet organizational goals but also positions the company to compete more effectively in today's dynamic job market. A diverse workforce allows organizations to draw from a richer talent pool, enhancing overall performance and productivity.

Another significant outcome of fostering diversity and inclusion is the creation of a positive organizational culture. Cultivating respect, equity, and inclusion nurtures a culture of trust, collaboration, and mutual support. When employees feel that they are treated fairly and that their voices are heard, they are more likely to work toward common goals, contribute to a positive work environment, and engage in behaviors that support organizational success. A strong, inclusive culture encourages employees to bring their authentic selves to work, which leads to higher morale, improved collaboration, and increased trust between teams.

Finally, the impact of diversity and inclusion extends beyond the workplace, contributing to broader social and economic progress. Organizations that prioritize equity and inclusion play a vital role in reducing inequalities in society. By fostering environments where all individuals have equal opportunities, they help break down systemic barriers that limit access to education, employment, and upward mobility. As a result, these organizations contribute to more equitable communities where diverse perspectives are respected, and everyone has a fair shot at success. This, in turn, drives positive change, fostering social and economic growth that benefits entire communities.

In summary, embracing diversity and inclusion is not just a moral imperative—it's a strategic advantage that yields significant organizational and societal benefits. From enhancing creativity and innovation to improving employee engagement and retention, promoting diversity helps build stronger, more resilient organizations that are better positioned to thrive in an increasingly interconnected world.

In sum, diversity and inclusion are not just moral imperatives—they are essential drivers of organizational success, creativity, and long-term sustainability.

Address Systemic Barriers

- **Conquering Systemic Barriers**

Systemic barriers refer to the embedded structural obstacles that limit opportunities enjoyed by persons in contrast with their marginalization. The several systemic barriers instituted within the hiring and education and health employment practices of persons further allow unequal opportunities to occur within growth and promotions. Overcoming these obstacles involves tearing down such structures and hindrances toward true equality and equitable opportunities and can be made possible only through a deliberate comprehensive process.

Identifying Systemic Barriers

Provide comprehensive audits that identify areas where inequities are persistent, indicating system barriers. Systematic inequities in key systems may, in part, be brought about by hiring practices encumbered with biases in decision-making. For example, limited diversity within the leadership group may signal exclusionary practices in hiring. Similarly, access to education and healthcare can be limited by inequalities in funding, availability, or geographic access. Audits should focus on a basis of data gathering, listening to affected communities, and assessing the policies upholding these barriers.

Equitable Policy Support

Following the identification of systemic barriers, the next important area involves supporting policies that break down inequities. This may include advocating anti-discrimination laws and other regulations that ensure equal opportunity in employment, education, and health. Every organization and institution should make an effort to review policies and procedures with a view to ensuring that they are in no way perpetuating the inequality. Promoting Equitable Policies: Not only does this prevent discrimination, but it also creates environments where everyone gets an equal opportunity to excel.

Investing in initiatives that provide access to resources like healthcare, education, and employment equitably is essential. Such are initiatives within the community that address scholarship, training, mentorship, and available housing or child care. By targeted investments in underrepresented communities, people will have the tools they need to succeed, and opportunities, particularly in areas of disparities. This leads to a significant increase in overcoming barriers when resources are shared more equitably.

Why It Matters

The elimination of systemic barriers does not just offer equal opportunity but rather fairness and an atmosphere that is conducive and allows all people to be successful, regardless of background. When systemic barriers no longer exist, then there are opportunities for marginalized groups to acquire opportunities that were otherwise denied to them, creating a more socially and economically mobile society. This will help in making a society that is more inclusive, where everyone has opportunities to realize their full potential. Eventually, eliminating systemic barriers guarantees fairness, reduces disparities, and contributes to a future with more justice and equality.

Provide Equal Access to Resources

Equity is the opportunity given to all people to have the tools, resources, and opportunities to be successful, regardless of their background or identity. Equity fundamentally removes barriers so that everyone has a fair shot at reaching their goals.

In essence, successfully introducing equity into practice calls for the taking of focused steps on behalf of an organization or community by providing for systems of support. These range from mentorship programs intended to shepherd underrepresented groups and scholarships to help students overcome economic disadvantages, to professional development in support of elevation up a career path. As we begin to invest this way, so we begin to forge a pathway along which others might travel in their desire to achieve their full potentials in contribution.

Besides, investment in community programs addressing basic needs around affordable housing, healthcare, and childcare is important. These programs deal with both short-term problems and ultimately bear fruits in the long run since individuals can thereafter be able to achieve some permanency and security in their lives. People who have affordable housing, necessary healthcare, and reliable childcare will then be prepared to attend to other personal and professional interests.

Equally importantly, resources and funding will have to be equitably distributed. Ensuring fair allocation based on need rather than privilege can help address entrenched disparities across various sectors that have prevailed in education, employment, and social welfare. If this distribution does not take place, systemic inequality will persist and continue to create disadvantage for marginalized groups.

Where there are disparities in the providing of resources, let's identify and try to make certain this level the playing field. It is easy to see that reducing inequalities will not only benefit the individuals but also contribute to a generally healthier, more just society where all can prosper and be successful.

Foster Education and Awareness

Education stands as one of the most powerful tools for raising awareness about equity and fostering a deeper understanding of systemic issues. At its core, education equips individuals with the knowledge and skills necessary to recognize disparities and address them meaningfully. By focusing on equity and inclusion, educational initiatives play a critical role in dismantling prejudices and promoting a culture of fairness and justice.

Several key approaches can be employed to effectively implement education as a strategy for promoting equity. First, developing comprehensive educational programs that center around equity, diversity, and inclusion is essential. These programs should not only provide theoretical knowledge but also offer practical insights into how biases manifest in everyday life and institutional structures. Schools, workplaces, and community organizations should prioritize these educational initiatives, ensuring they are accessible to all.

In addition to creating educational programs, it's crucial to provide resources and training aimed at enhancing cultural competency and addressing unconscious bias. Cultural competency involves understanding, respecting, and appreciating the diverse backgrounds, experiences, and perspectives of others. Through workshops, seminars, and online courses, individuals can develop the skills needed to recognize their biases and work toward eliminating them. Training on unconscious bias helps individuals become more self-aware, thereby reducing the likelihood of perpetuating discriminatory behaviors.

Open dialogue and discussion play a vital role in fostering an environment where equity issues can be explored and addressed openly. Encouraging honest conversations about race, gender, socioeconomic status, and other factors that contribute to inequality is critical. Safe spaces for dialogue allow individuals to share experiences, listen to others, and gain a deeper understanding of the challenges faced by marginalized communities. These conversations, when conducted in good faith, can break down barriers, bridge gaps, and inspire collective action toward equity.

The importance of education in promoting equity cannot be overstated. Educated individuals are more likely to recognize unfair practices, challenge systemic inequalities, and advocate for policies that support inclusivity. Knowledge empowers people to not only understand the root causes of inequity but also to take intentional steps toward creating a more just society. Informed individuals contribute to a culture of respect, empathy, and fairness, helping to dismantle oppressive

structures and build environments where everyone has an equal opportunity to succeed.

Promote Fair Policies and Practices

Fair policies play a crucial role in promoting equity by ensuring that individuals are not marginalized or excluded due to their identity, background, or personal circumstances. These policies serve as the foundation for creating an inclusive environment where everyone has equal access to opportunities and resources.

How to Implement Fair Policies

To begin, it's essential to review organizational policies to ensure they are unbiased and inclusive. This means evaluating every aspect of the workplace—from recruitment and hiring processes to promotions, benefits, and access to resources. Biases can often be subtle, so conducting comprehensive audits helps identify areas where exclusion or unequal treatment may occur. For example, policies on hiring, performance evaluations, and career advancement should be scrutinized to eliminate any practices that disproportionately affect certain groups.

In addition to internal audits, advocating for laws and regulations that protect against discrimination is equally important. Policies that uphold equal treatment and prohibit discriminatory practices are essential for creating equitable environments. This could involve supporting or implementing legislation that ensures fair pay, equal opportunities for leadership roles, and protection against biases such as race, gender, age, or disability discrimination. Encouraging legislative measures at local, national, or even international levels helps establish the legal frameworks necessary to uphold equity.

Furthermore, organizations must establish frameworks that hold themselves accountable for equity goals. Setting clear objectives, tracking progress, and creating mechanisms to evaluate the impact of policies ensures transparency and responsibility. This involves not only measuring outcomes but also fostering a culture of accountability. For instance, diversity and inclusion audits, feedback mechanisms, and periodic reviews ensure that policies remain practical and reflective of an organization's commitment to fairness.

Why Fair Policies Matter

Fair policies play a vital role in building a level playing field where everyone has the opportunity to succeed. They help dismantle systemic barriers by addressing and mitigating inequalities that can otherwise persist. When policies are designed with equity in mind, they foster environments where all individuals, regardless of their background, feel valued, respected, and included.

Moreover, organizations that prioritize fair policies tend to benefit from enhanced innovation, creativity, and productivity. A diverse and equitable workplace is more likely to attract top talent, as individuals are drawn to environments that support fairness and growth. In turn, this contributes to a stronger sense of trust, loyalty, and belonging, which are essential for fostering a positive organizational culture.

Ultimately, fair policies are not just about compliance or meeting external standards; they are about creating a foundation for long-term, sustainable equity. By ensuring that no one is left behind due to their identity, organizations can cultivate an environment where every individual has the chance to thrive.

Engage Communities and Empower Individuals

Empowering individuals and communities to lead equity efforts is essential to promoting fairness and inclusivity. This approach recognizes that actual change often comes from those who are directly affected by inequities. When communities are empowered, they can drive their solutions and advocate for their needs, leading to long-term progress.

To effectively implement this, it's essential to actively involve community members in decision-making and leadership roles. This ensures that their voices are heard and respected, helping to shape policies and initiatives that directly address their unique challenges. By giving communities, the power to influence decisions that impact their lives, we move toward a more inclusive and equitable future.

Another critical strategy is supporting grassroots movements that focus on equity. These movements often emerge from within communities and are driven by those who have firsthand experience with systemic barriers. By providing resources, funding, and platforms for these groups to amplify their efforts, we validate their experiences and empower them to push for meaningful change.

Additionally, it is vital to provide communities with the tools and resources they need to address their unique challenges. These may include access to education, funding, healthcare, or infrastructure. When communities are equipped with the necessary resources, they can develop tailored solutions that address the specific barriers they face, fostering resilience and self-sufficiency.

The importance of this approach lies in the fact that empowered communities can create lasting change. When people feel a sense of ownership and control over the decisions that affect their lives, they are more motivated to sustain efforts and continue advocating for equity. Empowerment leads to stronger collaboration, greater trust, and a collective commitment to long-term justice and fairness, ensuring that equity becomes a lasting part of society's fabric.

Promoting equity requires intentional effort and a commitment to creating a fair and just environment. By embracing diversity, addressing systemic barriers, providing access to resources, and fostering education, we can move toward a more equitable society. Each small action contributes to more extensive, lasting change, ensuring that everyone has the opportunity to thrive.

LEADERSHIP'S ROLE

Leadership plays a critical role in shaping the values, norms, and behaviors that define an organization's culture. Leaders' attitudes and actions set the tone for how diversity, equity, and inclusion are prioritized within a workplace. Effective leaders serve not only as decision-makers but also as role models who influence the way employees interact, collaborate, and perceive one another.

The Influence of Leadership in Shaping Workplace Culture

Leadership sets the foundation for an inclusive and equitable workplace by establishing clear expectations and norms that promote respect and fairness. When leaders actively promote diversity, they send a powerful message that all employees are valued, regardless of their background. For instance, leaders who demonstrate respect for differing opinions, encourage open dialogue and ensure that marginalized voices are heard contribute to a culture of acceptance. Conversely, leaders who remain silent on issues of equity or fail to address biases can inadvertently foster a workplace environment where exclusionary practices persist. By prioritizing values such as fairness, empathy, and respect, leaders help to create a culture where employees feel safe, supported, and motivated to contribute their best work.

Moreover, leadership plays a crucial role in holding teams accountable for diversity and inclusion goals. Leaders are responsible for monitoring and measuring progress, addressing any inequities, and taking actionable steps to rectify disparities. When leaders demonstrate their commitment to equity through both their words and actions, they inspire employees to adopt similar values, creating a ripple effect throughout the organization. This ensures that diversity and inclusion are not merely theoretical concepts but are actively embedded into the day-to-day operations of the workplace.

How Leaders Can Model Inclusivity

Leaders have a unique opportunity to model inclusivity through their behaviors, communication, and decision-making. One of the most effective ways leaders can demonstrate inclusivity is by fostering an open and respectful communication environment. They can encourage active listening, where all voices are heard and valued. This means creating opportunities for diverse perspectives to be shared in meetings, brainstorming sessions, and decision-making processes. By listening attentively and showing that everyone's input matters, leaders set a tone of inclusivity that empowers employees to feel confident in expressing themselves.

Another key aspect of modeling inclusivity is acknowledging and addressing unconscious biases. Leaders must take steps to become self-aware of their own biases and actively work to eliminate them. By recognizing these biases, leaders can create policies and practices that ensure fairness in recruitment, promotions, and performance evaluations. For example, adopting blind recruitment processes, implementing diverse interview panels, and ensuring fair salary structures are all ways leaders can help dismantle barriers to equity.

Leaders also contribute to an inclusive workplace by advocating for the representation of underrepresented groups in leadership positions. By actively promoting individuals from diverse backgrounds into higher roles, leaders signal their commitment to fostering equality and opening doors for others. This not only strengthens organizational leadership by bringing in a broader range of experiences but also inspires employees from marginalized groups, showing them that their voices and talents are valued.

Additionally, leaders can model inclusivity by creating policies and practices that reflect a commitment to flexibility, work-life balance, and well-being. Providing equitable opportunities for remote work, flexible schedules, and support systems for underrepresented groups can further promote inclusivity. Leaders who prioritize equity and fairness in these areas contribute to a workplace culture where employees feel they can thrive without sacrificing their identity or well-being.

Ultimately, leaders play a pivotal role in shaping organizational culture. By leading with integrity, empathy, and a commitment to equity, they set the stage for a more inclusive workplace where everyone has the opportunity to succeed. Modeling inclusivity ensures that the principles of diversity, equity, and inclusion become embedded in the organization's core values, making them an integral part of the workplace rather than just a goal to aspire toward.

INTERVENTIONS THAT WORK

Addressing bias in workplaces and institutions is no easy feat, but specific interventions have proven effective when designed thoughtfully. By combining bias training programs with structural changes, organizations can create fairer and more inclusive environments. Here's how these interventions can make a difference:

Bias Training Programs: What Works and What Doesn't

Bias training is often the first step organizations take to address unconscious bias. However, not all programs are equally effective. Let's explore what works and what doesn't:

What Works:

Enhancing Bias Training for Meaningful Change

Bias training is most effective when it goes beyond surface-level discussions to deeply engage participants, fostering genuine understanding and behavioral transformation. Interactive methods, ongoing reinforcement, evidence-based content, and safe spaces for dialogue are key elements that make such training impactful.

One of the most potent approaches involves incorporating real-world examples into the training. When participants engage with scenarios, role-playing activities, and case studies that mirror actual workplace situations, they are more likely to recognize bias as it manifests in practical settings. This interactive approach moves beyond theory, helping individuals see how bias can influence decisions and relationships. By experiencing these dynamics in a controlled environment, participants learn strategies to counteract bias and build healthier habits that carry into their everyday interactions.

However, for training to be truly transformative, it cannot be a one-time event. A single workshop may create initial awareness, but deep-seated biases require ongoing efforts to challenge and change. Successful programs incorporate a continuum of learning that includes follow-up sessions, periodic refreshers, and reinforcement activities. This sustained engagement ensures that participants not only retain what they've learned but also adapt their behaviors over time. It's a long-term investment in fostering a bias-aware culture that continually improves.

Another critical aspect is grounding the training in robust, evidence-based content. Programs built on psychological and sociological research provide participants with actionable insights that are proven to work. By linking training content to studies and real-world outcomes, organizations can ensure their efforts are both credible and compelling. Evidence-based training avoids guesswork and delivers strategies that align with human behavior, making it more likely that participants will internalize and apply what they learn.

Creating an environment where participants feel safe to engage is equally essential. Bias is a sensitive and deeply personal topic, and encouraging open conversations allows individuals to share their experiences without fear of judgment. When people feel heard and understood, empathy flourishes, and biases are often softened. These safe spaces foster connections between colleagues, helping participants see past stereotypes and build a deeper appreciation for diverse perspectives.

By weaving these elements into bias training programs, organizations can create a holistic experience that raises awareness and inspires meaningful change. Through thoughtful design and consistent reinforcement, bias training becomes a powerful tool for cultivating a workplace culture rooted in inclusivity, understanding, and mutual respect.

What Doesn't Work:

Shaming or blaming participants during bias training is counterproductive and often leads to defensiveness and resistance. When individuals are made to feel guilty or judged for their biases, they may become more focused on protecting their self-image rather than engaging with the material. This approach not only alienates participants but also undermines the ultimate goal of fostering understanding and promoting change.

Effective training takes a growth-oriented perspective, emphasizing solutions and practical strategies that encourage participants to recognize and address biases constructively. By framing the conversation around improvement and shared goals, organizations create an environment where employees feel supported in their efforts to unlearn prejudices.

Another common pitfall in bias training is overloading participants with information. While data, statistics, and theories are valuable, an excess of these without clear, practical applications can overwhelm and disengage participants. Training sessions that bombard attendees with academic concepts or dense materials often fail to resonate because they lack relevance to everyday experiences. For bias training to be impactful, it must include relatable examples, interactive components, and actionable steps. These elements help participants connect with the content, retain what they learn, and apply it effectively in real-world situations.

Finally, a critical misstep in addressing bias is focusing solely on individual behavior while ignoring systemic inequalities. Bias training that treats prejudice as an isolated, personal issue misses the larger picture of how structural biases are embedded in organizational systems and practices. While it is important to challenge and change individual attitudes, this alone cannot address the institutional barriers that perpetuate inequality. Comprehensive bias training must also examine and propose solutions for systemic issues, such as hiring practices, promotion criteria, and workplace policies, to create meaningful and sustainable change. By addressing both personal and structural biases, organizations can foster a truly inclusive culture.

Structural Changes to Minimize Bias

Structural interventions address bias at the organizational level, ensuring that systems and processes promote equity. Here are some proven strategies:

Blind Hiring:

Removing identifiers such as names, genders, and addresses from resumes is a simple yet powerful strategy to prevent unconscious bias during the initial stages of hiring. By eliminating personal details that might inadvertently trigger preconceived notions, this approach shifts the focus to the most critical aspects of a candidate's application: their skills, experience, and qualifications.

For example, a groundbreaking study conducted in Australia revealed the impact of anonymizing resumes on hiring outcomes. When resumes were stripped of personal identifiers, the likelihood of minority candidates being shortlisted for interviews increased by nearly 30%. This striking result demonstrates how unconscious biases can significantly influence hiring decisions and how anonymization effectively levels the playing field.

By focusing solely on merit, this practice ensures that hiring managers evaluate applicants based on their professional potential rather than assumptions tied to their identity or background. Beyond fairness, anonymized resumes enrich organizational diversity by uncovering talent that might otherwise be overlooked. The result is a stronger, more inclusive workforce that benefits from diverse perspectives and ideas.

1. **Diverse Interview Panels:**

Diversity in an interview panel nurtures a wide range of viewpoints that are very important in preventing or minimizing biases and assuring fairness in decision-making. The interviewers bring a lot of experiences, cultural understanding, and viewpoint to the table and hence be apt to question assumptions and realize any blind spots in making their evaluation. Diversity of thought ensures prevention from groupthink-that lack of divergence in opinions may lead to narrow or skewed judgments.

The diverse panel acts as a sign to the candidates that this organization embraces diversity and thus is attractive to the best talent irrespective of background. Decision-making also becomes balanced and fair since the process takes into consideration multiple perspectives, allowing the panel members to assess the candidates holistically. Each panelist might notice strengths or areas of potential that others may overlook, making the assessment richer and more accurate.

In the end, the panels make a merit-based hire, in congruence with organizational values and not unconscious preferences. This approach not only makes the process fair but also reinforces the organization's commitment toward the development of an inclusive and representative workforce.

Standardized Evaluation Criteria:

Using clear, predefined metrics for evaluating performance or potential minimizes subjectivity. By focusing on measurable outcomes, biases are less likely to creep into the process.

- **Encouraging Diverse Leadership:**

Organizations are key drivers toward promoting diversity, equity, and inclusion. They should be active in offering mentorship and sponsorship opportunities to underrepresented groups. Mentorship is more than networking; it is a structured way in which individuals of diverse backgrounds can seek guidance, resources, and support in their professional development. Mentorship offers employees the chance to learn about organizational culture, develop important skills, and receive personal tips that will help accelerate their growth. It is sponsorship that takes it up a notch by pairing the employees with influential advocates, the ones who actively champion an employee's advancement through open opportunities for promotions and leading roles.

These actions do much more than impact only those individuals who participate directly in them. When an organization supports diverse talent visibly and gives it priority through mentorship or sponsorship, it sends a strong message about inclusivity that permeates the workforce. Employees are motivated by seeing leadership that reflects diverse backgrounds, life experiences, and perspectives. This representative inclusion fosters a feeling of fit, but at the same time, it challenges those deeply held stereotypes about who is "qualified" to lead.

Longer term, these initiatives can create organizational cultural shifts: more diverse perspectives in decision-making, creative problem solving, and deeper relationships with clients and communities. It shows that success opportunities are available to all and provides a working environment in which employees feel valued and empowered to give their best. Development of a diverse pipeline of future leaders means an organization is not only making amends for past inequities but also positioning itself for a better and more prosperous future.

- **Accountability and Transparency:**

Regular assessment and publication of information in key areas like hiring, promotion, and salary scales are an integral feature of any accountability process at firms. Such a record provides companies with indications of where disparities or trends in practices can occur that, unbeknownst to them, further discrimination in non-intentional ways. For example, hiring data analysis may reveal underrepresentation at different levels, while pay equity audits may show salary gaps that need to be bridged.

Equally important is transparency in the process. When organizations share their findings openly with employees, stakeholders, and the public, they are being fair and inclusive. This openness will not only breed trust among employees, who will feel confident that their contributions are valued equitably, but also present the organization as one that takes ethical practices seriously. Moreover, this level of visibility creates natural motivation for continuous improvement: the very sharing of data encourages companies to review the progress and fine-tune strategies periodically.

In the long run, this continuous assessment of data and transparency combine to ensure accountability, fairness, and shared responsibility in developing an equitable workplace.

Why These Interventions Matter

Bias harms individuals and affects the entire organization by limiting innovation, morale, and trust. Combining effective bias training programs with structural changes creates a powerful strategy to tackle bias from both individual and systemic angles.

By investing in these interventions, organizations can build stronger, more inclusive teams where everyone has an equal opportunity to thrive.

PART IV: MOVING FORWARD: MEASURING SUCCESS IN DIVERSITY, EQUITY, AND INCLUSION (DEI)

Creating a more inclusive and equitable environment is a continuous journey that requires intentional effort, reflection, and a clear understanding of progress. Measuring success in diversity, equity, and inclusion (DEI) is essential to ensure that initiatives are effective and aligned with the goals of reducing bias and fostering an inclusive culture. But how do we track progress and honestly know when we're making a difference? Let's break it down.

Tracking Progress in Reducing Bias

Addressing bias, whether conscious or unconscious, is at the heart of any DEI initiative. Success in reducing bias can be observed through tangible and intangible markers. Here are practical ways to track progress:

1. **Anonymous Surveys and Feedback**

Regularly distributing anonymous surveys to employees, stakeholders, or participants serves as a powerful tool for gathering honest feedback and gauging the effectiveness of diversity, equity, and inclusion (DEI) efforts. These surveys create a safe space for individuals to voice their experiences, concerns, and perceptions without fear of repercussions, ensuring the authenticity of the responses.

To maximize the impact of these surveys, the questions should be thoughtfully designed to address key areas that reflect the organization's culture and progress in DEI. For example, survey questions can explore:

- **Sense of Respect**: Do individuals feel respected and valued by their peers, managers, and the organization as a whole? Are diverse perspectives welcomed and appreciated?

- **Fair Treatment**: Are individuals treated equitably, regardless of their background, gender, race, or other characteristics?

- **Decision-Making Processes**: Do respondents perceive bias in hiring, promotions, or resource allocation? Are decisions made transparently and fairly?

- **Belonging and Inclusion**: Do employees feel a sense of belonging? Are they able to bring their authentic selves to work without fear of judgment or exclusion?

To gain deeper insights, consider incorporating open-ended questions that allow respondents to elaborate on their experiences. For instance:

- "Can you describe a specific situation where you felt particularly included or excluded in the workplace?"

- "What changes would you recommend to improve fairness and inclusivity in decision-making processes?"

The frequency of these surveys also matters. Quarterly or biannual surveys provide timely data while allowing enough time for initiatives to take effect. Additionally, pairing survey results with demographic data (collected anonymously and ethically) can reveal trends and disparities among different groups, offering actionable insights for targeted interventions.

It's equally important to act on the feedback received. Sharing aggregated results with employees and outlining the steps the organization plans to take based on the findings demonstrates a genuine commitment to progress. This not only builds trust but also ensures that employees feel their voices are heard and valued in shaping an inclusive workplace.

2. **Monitoring Workplace Behavior**

Changes in behavior serve as a powerful indicator of progress when addressing bias and fostering an inclusive environment. Observable shifts, such as increased collaboration across diverse teams, more open and respectful communication, or a noticeable reduction in complaints related to discrimination, signal that efforts to reduce bias are taking root. These changes highlight a growing sense of trust and belonging among individuals, which are key markers of a healthy, inclusive culture.

To achieve and sustain these shifts, training programs focused on bias awareness are essential. However, the accurate measure of success lies not only in the completion of these programs but in how they influence day-to-day interactions and decision-making. Organizations should take a proactive approach to evaluate the impact of such training. This can be achieved by:

1. **Post-Training Assessments:** Conducting surveys or interviews shortly after training sessions to gather feedback on participants' understanding and awareness. Questions should aim to uncover how the training has shaped their perception of bias and influenced their behavior.

2. **Behavioral Observations:** Assigning managers or team leaders to observe interactions within their teams and provide qualitative feedback. Look for signs of increased inclusivity, such as more equitable participation in meetings or the willingness to challenge stereotypes constructively.

3. **Monitoring Key Metrics:** Tracking data on workplace incidents, such as grievances related to discrimination or conflicts, to identify trends over time. A steady decline in such incidents can indicate a positive cultural shift.

4. **Encouraging Peer Accountability:** Fostering an environment where team members feel empowered to hold each other accountable for biased behavior. Introducing mechanisms like anonymous reporting or peer review systems can promote this culture of mutual responsibility.

5. **Follow-Up Activities:** Reinforcing training with follow-up workshops, interactive discussions, or team-building exercises to keep the focus on bias awareness and ensure it becomes ingrained in organizational practices.

6. **Celebrating Progress:** Recognizing and celebrating milestones, such as successful collaborations across diverse groups or innovative solutions developed through inclusive teamwork, can reinforce positive behaviors and motivate ongoing improvement.

By combining training with consistent observation, feedback, and reinforcement, organizations can ensure that changes in behavior are not just temporary shifts but lasting transformations. Over time, these efforts create a ripple effect, fostering an environment where inclusion and equity become second nature, ultimately driving greater engagement, innovation, and success.

3. Reviewing Recruitment and Retention Data

Reducing bias is a multifaceted effort that starts with creating fair, inclusive hiring practices and continues with strategies to retain and support diverse talent over time. A holistic approach ensures that every step of the employee lifecycle, from recruitment to retention, is free from bias and fosters equity. Here's how organizations can tackle these critical components:

Fair Hiring Practices

Building an unbiased hiring process begins with examining how job opportunities are presented, and candidates are evaluated. Key steps include:

1. Crafting Inclusive Job Descriptions

Avoid using language that may unintentionally deter underrepresented groups. For example, overly aggressive terms like "ninja" or "rockstar" may alienate specific candidates. Instead, use clear, welcoming language that emphasizes the skills and values sought.

2. Standardizing Hiring Processes

Implement structured interviews with pre-determined questions and evaluation criteria to reduce subjective judgments. This approach ensures all candidates are assessed on the same scale, based on skills and experience relevant to the role.

3. **Broadening Recruitment Channels**

Actively source candidates from diverse backgrounds by partnering with organizations, universities, and platforms that focus on underrepresented groups. This helps expand the pool of talent and reduces reliance on referrals that may perpetuate homogeneity.

4. **Training for Unconscious Bias**

Provide hiring managers and recruitment teams with ongoing training to recognize and mitigate unconscious biases that may influence decisions during the hiring process.

5. **Analyzing Recruitment Data**

Regularly track metrics such as the diversity of applicants, interviewees, and hires. These data points can reveal trends and highlight potential areas of bias, such as bottlenecks where candidates from specific backgrounds are disproportionately eliminated.

Retention and Development of Diverse Talent

Hiring diverse employees is only the first step; retaining and nurturing them is equally critical. A strong focus on retention ensures that talent from all backgrounds feels supported, valued, and empowered to grow. Key strategies include:

1. **Creating an Inclusive Workplace Culture**

Foster a culture where employees feel respected, heard, and valued. Encourage open communication and provide platforms for employees to share their experiences and ideas without fear of reprisal.

2. **Offering Growth and Development Opportunities**

Provide equitable access to training, mentorship, and career advancement programs. Tailored professional development initiatives can help underrepresented employees build their skills and prepare for leadership roles.

3. **Regularly Reviewing Retention Metrics**

Analyze turnover rates by demographic groups to identify disparities. Exit interviews and surveys can offer valuable insights into why employees leave and whether bias or inequities contribute to their decisions.

4. **Promoting Pay and Performance Equity**

Conduct routine audits to ensure that employees performing similar roles are compensated equitably. Address any disparities in pay, promotions, or performance evaluations that may disproportionately affect underrepresented groups.

5. **Establishing Affinity Groups and Support Networks**

Encourage the formation of employee resource groups (ERGs) or affinity groups that provide support, networking, and advocacy for diverse employees. These groups can also act as valuable resources for organizational leaders to understand the unique challenges faced by their members.

Connecting Recruitment and Retention Efforts

A key to reducing bias lies in integrating recruitment and retention strategies into a unified framework. For example:

- **Feedback Loops**: Insights from retention metrics, such as turnover rates or engagement surveys, can inform improvements to hiring practices. If diverse employees are leaving due to a lack of growth opportunities, the recruitment team can prioritize candidates who align with long-term growth initiatives.

- **Celebrating Success**: Sharing stories of diverse employees who have grown within the organization can inspire new hires and reinforce a culture of inclusion.

By continuously refining hiring practices and focusing on retention, organizations can create an environment where diverse talent not only enters but thrives. This holistic approach demonstrates a genuine commitment to equity and inclusion, ensuring a sustainable, bias-free workplace for all.

4. **Incorporating Bias Interruption Strategies**

Establishing mechanisms to interrupt bias is a proactive and critical step in fostering fairness and equity within any organization. These mechanisms serve as guardrails, ensuring that unconscious biases do not influence decision-making processes. Examples include **structured decision-making tools**, which provide a clear framework for evaluating candidates, projects, or policies based on objective criteria. Similarly, **checklists** act as reminders to evaluate decisions through an equity-focused lens, reducing the likelihood of overlooking underrepresented voices or perspectives.

Another powerful approach is incorporating **diverse hiring panels** that include individuals from various backgrounds, experiences, and perspectives. This not only helps counteract biases during recruitment but also ensures that decisions reflect diverse viewpoints.

To maximize the effectiveness of these strategies, **periodic reviews** of the tools and mechanisms in place are essential. These reviews should assess their real-world impact, gathering data to identify successes and areas needing improvement. For example, tracking whether structured tools consistently result in more equitable hiring decisions or whether diverse panels lead to more inclusive outcomes can provide actionable insights.

Additionally, organizations can seek feedback from participants who interact with these mechanisms to understand their experiences and refine processes accordingly. By maintaining a commitment to continuous improvement, these bias-interruption strategies not only minimize biases but also help embed equity and fairness into the organization's culture and operations.

Key Performance Indicators (KPIs) for Diversity, Equity, and Inclusion

To effectively measure DEI efforts, organizations must define clear KPIs tailored to their specific goals. These KPIs serve as benchmarks for assessing progress and identifying areas for improvement. Examples include:

1. **Representation Metrics**

Workforce Demographics: Tracking the representation of employees from underrepresented groups across all levels of an organization is a cornerstone of creating a truly inclusive workplace. This process involves examining not just the overall percentage of diverse employees but also their distribution throughout the organizational hierarchy. Often, diversity is concentrated in entry-level roles, with representation diminishing as you move up to senior leadership positions. Addressing this imbalance requires a deeper understanding of the factors contributing to these gaps.

Organizations need to approach this analysis holistically by evaluating the entire talent pipeline. This means looking at hiring practices to ensure job postings and recruitment efforts are reaching diverse talent pools while also examining internal promotion systems to identify barriers that may prevent equitable career advancement. For instance, are decision-making processes unintentionally favoring certain groups? Are mentorship and leadership development opportunities accessible to all employees?

Another vital aspect is benchmarking. Comparing your organization's representation metrics to industry standards can provide valuable context, helping you gauge progress and identify areas for improvement. However, it's not just about meeting benchmarks; it's about going beyond them to create an environment where all individuals, regardless of background, feel empowered to succeed.

Tracking representation also requires a commitment to long-term goals. Organizations must set clear targets for improving diversity at all levels and regularly measure progress. Transparency in sharing these metrics, both internally and externally, demonstrates accountability and reinforces a culture of trust and inclusion.

It's equally important to consider retention. Representation is not just about who you hire but who stays. If employees from underrepresented groups are leaving at higher rates, it may signal issues with workplace culture, inclusion, or support systems. Addressing these challenges is vital to maintaining a truly representative workforce.

By taking a nuanced and proactive approach to track representation, organizations can ensure that diversity is not just a checkbox at the entry-level but a reality throughout every layer of their structure. This fosters a culture where equity is embedded in every opportunity, and every individual has the chance to thrive.

Applicant Pools: Monitoring the diversity of candidates applying for positions is a crucial step in fostering equitable hiring practices and building an inclusive workplace. This involves collecting demographic data from applicants in a voluntary, confidential, and compliant manner with privacy laws.

By doing so, organizations gain insights into how well their recruitment strategies are reaching underrepresented groups. For example, if specific demographics are consistently underrepresented in the applicant pool, it may indicate the need for a more inclusive approach to outreach and job postings.

One effective way to assess this is by analyzing candidate data at various stages of the hiring process. Tracking who applies advances to interviews and ultimately gets hired can highlight potential biases or systemic barriers within the process. For instance, if a disproportionately low number of candidates from certain groups advance past the initial screening, it may signal the need to review criteria or introduce bias-reducing measures, such as blind resume reviews.

The language used in job postings also plays a significant role in attracting diverse candidates. Inclusive, neutral wording that avoids unnecessary jargon or overly gendered language ensures the position appeals to a broader audience. Expanding recruitment channels to include partnerships with organizations and communities that support underrepresented groups can also help broaden the reach.

Setting measurable goals for candidate diversity and continuously refining recruitment strategies based on feedback and data is essential. For example, an organization might aim to increase the percentage of applications from women or ethnic minorities by a specific timeframe. Such targets encourage accountability and provide a clear framework for tracking progress.

By focusing on these efforts, organizations enhance the fairness of their hiring practices and create a workforce rich in perspectives, ideas, and innovation.

2. Engagement and Satisfaction

Employee Engagement Scores: Pulse surveys are powerful tools for understanding how included and valued employees feel in a workplace. Unlike lengthy annual surveys, pulse surveys are brief and conducted regularly, allowing organizations to capture real-time feedback on employee sentiments. By carefully crafting questions, these surveys can explore key areas like whether employees feel their contributions are recognized, whether they feel comfortable expressing their perspectives and whether they see opportunities for growth.

To be effective, pulse surveys must ensure anonymity to foster honest responses. Employees are more likely to provide candid feedback when they trust that their answers are protected. This data can then be analyzed to identify trends, track the effectiveness of diversity and inclusion initiatives, and uncover potential disparities across teams or demographic groups. For example, if certain groups consistently report feeling undervalued, it signals an area requiring immediate attention.

However, collecting data alone isn't enough. Organizations must act on the feedback by addressing concerns, implementing changes, and transparently communicating the results back to employees. This follow-through builds trust and reinforces the organization's commitment to creating an inclusive culture. Over time, recurring surveys help measure progress, celebrate achievements, and demonstrate that employee voices are driving meaningful change. By fostering this culture of listening and responsiveness, pulse surveys play a crucial role in improving workplace inclusion and ensuring employees feel genuinely valued.

- **Net Promoter Score (NPS)**:

One of the most telling indicators of a truly inclusive and supportive work environment is whether employees would recommend their workplace to others. This measure offers invaluable insight into the overall culture and can be a strong reflection of an organization's commitment to diversity, equity, and inclusion (DEI).

This can be assessed through tools like the **Employee Net Promoter Score (eNPS)**, which asks employees a simple yet powerful question: **"On a scale of 0-10, how likely are you to recommend our company as a great place to work?"** Employees are classified into three groups based on their responses:

- **Promoters (9-10)**: These are employees who are highly satisfied with their experience and are likely to advocate for the company. Their satisfaction can indicate a positive, inclusive work environment.

- **Passives (7-8)**: These employees are generally satisfied but are less likely to advocate strongly. They may be neutral or indifferent towards the company's culture, which suggests areas for potential improvement in engagement or inclusivity.

- **Detractors (0-6)**: These employees may be dissatisfied or disengaged. Their feedback could point to underlying issues with inclusivity, fairness, or other aspects of company culture that need to be addressed.

By calculating the eNPS (Promoters - Detractors), organizations can gauge overall employee sentiment and uncover potential areas for DEI improvement. A high eNPS generally signifies a positive work environment, while a low score highlights the need for changes to improve employee satisfaction and inclusivity.

Why It Reflects an Inclusive Culture

Employees who feel valued, respected, and heard are much more likely to recommend their workplace to others. When an organization fosters a culture where diversity is celebrated, equity is prioritized, and inclusion is embedded into everyday practices, employees experience a greater sense of belonging. This positive experience is often reflected in their willingness to promote the company to their peers.

If employees feel that their individual identity is respected and that the company makes an effort to address issues of bias, discrimination, and inequity, they are more likely to be vocal advocates. The reverse is also true: employees who feel excluded, marginalized, or overlooked are less likely to recommend their workplace and may even actively discourage others from joining.

The Power of Employee Advocacy

Employee recommendations can have a far-reaching impact on a company's culture and ability to attract top talent. When employees advocate for their workplace, they create a powerful network effect, drawing in like-minded individuals who value inclusivity and belonging. A strong eNPS score can also serve as a competitive advantage in recruitment, signaling to prospective candidates that the company is committed to creating a welcoming environment for all.

Additionally, a high willingness to recommend the workplace can lead to higher retention rates. Employees who feel proud of where they work and see themselves as part of a supportive community are more likely to stay, reducing turnover costs and maintaining a stable, engaged workforce.

Improving Employee Net Promoter Score for DEI

If the eNPS score indicates room for improvement, organizations can take proactive steps to address the underlying causes. Regular feedback loops, employee resource groups (ERGs), and transparent communication about DEI efforts can help improve the workplace environment. By engaging with employees and acting on their feedback, companies can create a culture that nurtures inclusion and builds trust.

Ultimately, measuring whether employees would recommend their workplace is not just about tracking numbers—it's about understanding the human experience within the organization and making the necessary changes to foster an environment where everyone feels they truly belong.

3. **Pay Equity and Promotion Rates**

In order to build a truly inclusive and equitable workplace, it's vital that organizations not only focus on diversity in hiring but also ensure that employees are fairly compensated and given equal opportunities for career advancement. Addressing salary equity and promoting diverse talent at all levels are crucial steps toward dismantling systemic bias and fostering a culture of fairness and opportunity for all.

Analyzing Salary Data for Pay Equity

Compensation plays a significant role in attracting and retaining talent, and disparities in pay can signal inequality within an organization. To ensure employees performing similar roles are compensated equitably, regardless of gender, race, or other factors, organizations need to undertake a thorough analysis of salary data. Here's how:

Conduct Regular Pay Audits

Organizations should regularly audit their salary data to identify any pay gaps between employees doing the same or similar work. These audits should examine the intersection of various factors, such as gender, race, and age, as well as the nature of the roles and any potential biases that could influence pay decisions.

Break Down the Data by Demographics

Salary audits should not only focus on raw salary figures but also consider bonuses, stock options, and other forms of compensation. By breaking down the data by demographic factors such as gender, race, disability, and other potentially impacted groups, organizations can gain a clearer picture of whether certain groups are being undervalued in comparison to their peers.

Analyze Compensation Trends Over Time

Pay disparities can also develop over time due to historical biases, so it's important to look at how compensation has evolved across different groups. A consistent trend where certain groups are consistently paid less, even after adjusting for experience and qualifications, could indicate underlying systemic bias.

Ensure Pay Transparency

Pay transparency is a key element in promoting fairness and accountability. Organizations that openly share their compensation structures and policies are more likely to build trust and prevent potential disparities from being hidden. While it may require a cultural shift, implementing pay transparency can help ensure that everyone in the organization understands how compensation is determined and can raise concerns if necessary.

Address Pay Inequities Promptly

Once any pay disparities are identified, organizations must take immediate action to address them. This may involve adjusting salaries to ensure they align with the market rate, qualifications, and experience for similar roles. By correcting these inequities, organizations not only demonstrate their commitment to fairness but also improve employee morale and retention.

Tracking Promotion Rates for Underrepresented Groups

Career advancement is another critical area where equity must be prioritized. If underrepresented groups face barriers to promotion or lack equal access to career advancement opportunities, it can perpetuate inequality within the organization. Here's how to ensure that promotion opportunities are distributed fairly:

Track Promotion Data by Demographics

Organizations should systematically track promotion rates across different demographic groups, such as gender, race, and other identity factors. This allows companies to identify whether certain groups are underrepresented in higher-level positions or if there are disparities in how frequently employees from different backgrounds are promoted.

Assess Promotion Criteria and Processes

Sometimes, the promotion process itself can be influenced by unconscious biases or a lack of clarity in how decisions are made. Organizations should regularly evaluate their promotion criteria to ensure they are transparent, objective, and based on merit. If informal networks or subjective factors (such as "cultural fit") are used in decision-making, it may unintentionally disadvantage underrepresented groups.

Implement Mentorship and Sponsorship Programs

Providing mentorship and sponsorship opportunities for employees from underrepresented groups can play a pivotal role in ensuring they have the support and guidance necessary to advance in their careers. Sponsorship, in particular, is about advocating for talented individuals to move into higher roles, which often leads to increased visibility and opportunity.

Focus on Leadership Development

One way to promote equal career advancement is to ensure that all employees, regardless of background, have access to leadership development programs. These programs should be designed to help individuals build the skills, network, and experience necessary to take on more senior roles. Specific programs tailored to address the needs of underrepresented groups can ensure these employees are not left behind in leadership pipelines.

Set Clear and Transparent Promotion Goals

Organizations can set goals to increase the representation of underrepresented groups in leadership positions by a certain date. These goals should be measurable, with progress tracked regularly and communicated to the team. Setting specific targets for promotions or leadership positions ensures that career advancement is actively pursued, rather than left to chance.

Foster an Inclusive Work Culture

Even with transparent policies and mentorship opportunities in place, career advancement can still be hindered if the workplace culture doesn't support diverse voices. Organizations need to cultivate an inclusive environment where employees from all backgrounds feel empowered to speak up, contribute ideas, and pursue leadership opportunities. Inclusive leadership practices, like actively listening to diverse perspectives and promoting a culture of respect, are essential to supporting career growth for all employees.

4. Training Completion and Impact

To gauge the success of DEI (Diversity, Equity, and Inclusion) training programs, it's essential to not only measure participation but also assess the depth of learning and behavioral change that result from the training. Here's how to expand and improve this process:

Measuring DEI Training Completion and Effectiveness

Track Participation Rates

The first step in measuring the success of a DEI training program is tracking the number of employees who have completed the training. This data is essential for understanding engagement levels and identifying any gaps in participation. By monitoring completion rates across different departments, teams, or demographic groups, organizations can ensure that the training reaches a broad and diverse audience. Additionally, it can highlight areas where additional efforts may be needed to encourage participation, such as providing incentives or ensuring access to the training during working hours.

Post-Training Assessments

Conduct post-training assessments to evaluate how well employees have absorbed the information presented during the training. These assessments can take the form of quizzes, surveys, or knowledge checks that test the understanding of key concepts such as unconscious bias, microaggressions, cultural competency, and inclusive leadership. By evaluating employees' grasp of the material, organizations can identify areas where the training content may need to be refined or expanded.

Feedback Surveys to Measure Perceived Impact

After training completion, gather feedback from participants through detailed surveys. These surveys should not only ask whether the training was practical but also delve deeper into how the training impacted employees' perceptions of diversity, equity, and inclusion in the workplace. Some key questions to include are:

- Did the training help you recognize unconscious biases in yourself or others?
- How confident do you feel in applying the concepts from the training in your day-to-day work?
- What actions will you take as a result of the training?
- Is the company actively fostering an inclusive environment based on what you learned?

The answers to these questions will help the employees better understand the training's effectiveness.

Behavioral Changes and Application of Learning

Beyond knowledge, the real goal of DEI training is to inspire action. Monitoring behavioral changes in the workplace post-training is crucial to understanding the actual impact. This can be tracked through employee feedback, supervisor observations, and changes in workplace dynamics. For example, has there been a noticeable improvement in how employees collaborate across diverse teams? Are individuals more proactive in addressing microaggressions or promoting inclusion during meetings? These observable behaviors can serve as valuable indicators of whether the training is translating into real-world change.

Long-Term Impact and Retention of Knowledge

DEI learning should not be a one-time event but an ongoing process. To measure the long-term effectiveness of the training, consider conducting follow-up surveys or assessments six months to a year after the training session. This helps determine whether the knowledge gained has been retained over time and continues to influence workplace behavior. Additionally, consider setting up periodic refresher courses to keep DEI principles at the forefront of employees' minds and reinforce key concepts.

Manager and Leadership Feedback

Since managers play a key role in driving DEI practices within their teams, it's essential to gather feedback from leadership about how well employees are applying the principles learned in the training. Managers can provide insight into whether employees are incorporating inclusive behaviors into their work or if further support is needed. This feedback is crucial for understanding whether the training has led to a shift in workplace culture and if it aligns with organizational DEI objectives.

Use Data to Improve Future Training

The data collected from participation rates, post-training assessments, surveys, and feedback should be used to continuously refine and improve future DEI training programs. For example, if many employees express that specific topics are unclear or challenging, the training content can be adjusted for greater clarity. If participation is lower in specific departments or demographic groups, tailored outreach or incentives can be introduced to ensure wider engagement.

By consistently measuring both the participation and the impact of DEI training, organizations can ensure they are not only meeting compliance standards but also fostering a truly inclusive and equitable environment that empowers all employees.

5. **Policy and Initiative Success**

Diversity, Equity, and Inclusion (DEI) programs are crucial for creating workplaces that reflect the richness of different backgrounds and perspectives. While these programs aim to promote a fair and inclusive environment, it's essential to assess their effectiveness to ensure they are genuinely making a difference. Two specific DEI initiatives—mentorship opportunities for underrepresented groups and affinity groups—have gained significant attention in recent years. By tracking participation rates and outcomes, organizations can evaluate their impact and make necessary adjustments for continuous improvement.

Mentorship Opportunities for Underrepresented Groups: Fostering Growth and Equity

Mentorship programs designed for underrepresented groups serve as a powerful tool for leveling the playing field, providing guidance, support, and access to networks that may have otherwise been unavailable. These programs are especially vital in industries where specific demographics are historically underrepresented, such as women in tech or people of color in leadership positions.

Tracking Participation Rates: One of the first steps in evaluating the impact of mentorship programs is tracking participation rates. High engagement levels suggest that the program is appealing and accessible to the targeted groups. It's essential to gather data on the number of individuals participating as both mentees and mentors, considering factors such as gender, race, and career level.

Monitoring the number of underrepresented employees participating in mentorship programs allows organizations to identify whether certain groups are more or less likely to engage. If, for example, women of color are underrepresented in a mentorship program, this might signal the need to adjust the outreach or structure of the program to better meet their needs.

- **Evaluating Outcomes:** Participation alone doesn't guarantee success—outcomes must be measured to understand the true impact of mentorship programs. Key metrics to track include:
- **Career Advancement:** Are mentees receiving promotions, pay raises, or increased responsibilities as a result of the mentorship? Tracking career progression is crucial in evaluating the program's effectiveness.

- **Skills Development:** Are mentees gaining specific skills that enhance their professional abilities? This could include leadership skills, technical competencies, or personal development.
- **Retention Rates:** Mentorship programs can play a significant role in retaining talent, particularly among underrepresented groups. A high retention rate among mentees compared to those who did not participate can demonstrate the program's value.
- **Network Expansion:** Many mentees report that mentorship helps them expand their professional network. This outcome can be assessed by tracking whether mentees are more engaged in industry events, conferences, or cross-departmental projects after participating.

The success of mentorship programs can often be seen in the increased confidence and visibility of individuals who were once overlooked, leading to more significant opportunities for advancement and recognition.

Affinity Groups: Building Community and Strengthening Support Networks

Affinity groups, also known as employee resource groups (ERGs), provide a platform for individuals with common interests, backgrounds, or identities to come together. These groups serve as safe spaces for members to share experiences, discuss challenges, and provide mutual support. They can also play a significant role in driving change within organizations by influencing policy, advocating for resources, and shaping workplace culture.

Tracking Participation Rates: The first metric to consider when evaluating the success of affinity groups is participation. Are employees actively involved in these groups? The number of members, the frequency of meetings, and the level of engagement in group activities (such as events, advocacy, or volunteering) can provide insights into the program's popularity. It's also important to track whether membership is inclusive—does the group have diversity within its ranks, and are there any barriers to entry for employees?

Evaluating Outcomes: The impact of affinity groups can be evaluated by examining several key outcomes:

Employee Well-Being and Engagement: Affinity groups often provide employees with a sense of belonging, reducing feelings of isolation. Surveys and feedback from participants can help gauge the emotional and social benefits, such as increased morale and a stronger connection to the company's mission.

Increased Advocacy and Awareness: Successful affinity groups advocate for policies or initiatives that benefit their members. Outcomes can be tracked by measuring the success of these advocacy efforts, such as changes in company policy, new benefits, or improved work-life balance options.

Professional Development: Many affinity groups offer members opportunities for professional development, such as workshops, networking events, or speaker sessions. Tracking how many members of affinity groups have advanced in their careers, taken on leadership roles, or acquired new skills is key to assessing their impact.

Cross-Group Collaboration: Affinity groups can foster greater collaboration across departments and functions. Tracking joint initiatives or partnerships between different groups within the organization can demonstrate the power of these communities in building an interconnected workplace.

Creating an Inclusive Feedback Loop

To truly measure the impact of DEI programs like mentorship opportunities and affinity groups, organizations should create a feedback loop that continuously informs improvements. Employee surveys, one-on-one interviews, and focus groups are all valuable tools for understanding participants' experiences and gathering suggestions for program enhancement. It's essential to create a culture where feedback is encouraged and valued, allowing for the development of more effective DEI strategies.

Tracking participation rates and outcomes of specific DEI programs, such as mentorship opportunities for underrepresented groups and affinity groups, allows organizations to evaluate their effectiveness and make informed adjustments. By monitoring engagement, career advancement, skills development, and retention rates, companies can identify which aspects of these programs are most impactful. The goal is not just to check the boxes on diversity but to create tangible, long-lasting benefits for employees and the organization as a whole. By doing so, companies can foster an inclusive and supportive environment where everyone has the opportunity to thrive.

6. **Leadership Accountability**

In today's rapidly evolving workplace, Diversity, Equity, and Inclusion (DEI) have become more than just buzzwords; they are core values that define a company's culture, success, and future growth. For leaders, the role they play in shaping a DEI-conscious environment is paramount. Setting DEI goals and tracking progress regularly ensures that these values aren't just discussed in theory but actively championed and lived out in every aspect of their leadership.

The Importance of Setting DEI Goals for Leaders

The first step toward fostering an inclusive environment is for leaders to set clear, measurable DEI goals. These goals should be specific, actionable, and aligned with the organization's overall values. Setting these goals isn't just about checking boxes but about creating an atmosphere where all employees feel heard, valued, and supported.

Championing Inclusive Practices: Leaders must take proactive steps to ensure they are not only talking the talk but walking the walk. This means incorporating inclusive practices in hiring, decision-making, team-building, and communication strategies. DEI goals include reducing bias in recruitment, increasing diversity in leadership positions, or implementing training programs that promote inclusivity.

Driving Positive Change: Leaders should be held accountable for driving DEI initiatives and making a measurable impact. They must go beyond superficial actions and aim for long-term, transformative change that creates a lasting impact on the team dynamics and organizational culture.

Enhancing Employee Engagement and Retention: Inclusive leaders are often those who make employees feel seen, heard, and appreciated. By setting DEI goals, leaders contribute to a healthier workplace culture, which enhances employee satisfaction, loyalty, and retention. When leaders prioritize DEI, it fosters a sense of belonging that can be felt throughout the entire team.

Tracking Progress Through Quarterly Reviews

Tracking DEI progress is essential for ensuring that goals aren't just set but actively pursued. This is where the concept of quarterly reviews comes into play. These reviews offer an opportunity for reflection, feedback, and adjustment. They allow leaders to evaluate their efforts, identify gaps, and make improvements.

Regular Reflection and Feedback: Quarterly reviews provide a structured approach to assess whether DEI goals are being met. During these reviews, leaders should be encouraged to reflect on their progress. Are they meeting the targets set? Are they fostering an environment where inclusivity thrives? Feedback from team members can offer invaluable insights into how leaders' actions are impacting the workplace.

Adjusting Strategies as Needed: DEI is a continuous journey, not a one-time achievement. If specific goals aren't being met, quarterly reviews provide the perfect opportunity to reevaluate and pivot. Leaders should be flexible in adjusting their strategies based on real-time feedback. For example, if a diversity hiring initiative isn't yielding diverse candidates, the review might prompt a revision of recruitment practices or the introduction of new training for hiring managers.

Celebrating Successes: Quarterly reviews aren't just about identifying gaps; they should also serve as a celebration of progress. Leaders should highlight achievements, no matter how small, and recognize the positive impact they've made on their teams. This not only reinforces the importance of DEI but also motivates the entire team to stay engaged in these efforts.

Are Leaders Championing Inclusive Practices and Driving Positive Change?

A critical component of tracking DEI progress is determining if leaders are genuinely championing inclusive practices. Simply setting goals isn't enough; leaders need to actively drive positive change, influencing their teams to adopt inclusive behaviors and mindsets.

Lead by Example: True leadership in DEI comes from modeling the behavior you want to see. Are leaders creating opportunities for underrepresented voices to be heard? Are they advocating for diversity in decision-making processes? Leaders should consistently embody inclusive behavior, showing their teams what inclusivity looks like in practice.

Employee Perception: How do employees perceive their leaders when it comes to DEI? Are they seen as champions of inclusivity, or is there a disconnect between their words and actions? This can be gauged through surveys, interviews, and open forums. Employee sentiment is a powerful indicator of whether leaders are living up to their DEI commitments.

Building a Culture of Accountability: Leaders who champion inclusivity also create a culture of accountability. They hold themselves and others responsible for promoting diversity and inclusion. This includes addressing any biases or discriminatory behaviors that arise and ensuring that all employees are treated with respect and dignity.

Setting DEI goals for leaders and tracking their progress through regular reviews is essential for creating a diverse, equitable, and inclusive workplace. By taking these steps, organizations can ensure that their leaders are not just checking off goals but are actively driving meaningful change. These efforts help foster a work environment where all employees feel valued, heard, and supported, which ultimately leads to greater success, innovation, and growth for the entire organization. Remember, DEI is a journey, and with each goal set and review completed, leaders take one more step toward building a workplace that truly celebrates diversity, equity, and inclusion.

Why Measurement Matters

When we talk about Diversity, Equity, and Inclusion (DEI), the first thing that often comes to mind is the numbers. How many women, minorities, and people from underrepresented groups are in leadership positions? What's the gender pay gap? These figures certainly matter, but measuring DEI success goes much deeper than just statistics. True DEI success is a reflection of an organization's commitment to transparency, accountability, and, most importantly, creating an environment where every individual feels they truly belong.

It's Not About Checking Boxes; It's About Creating a Culture of Belonging

Success in DEI isn't about ticking off a checklist of initiatives or quotas. While tracking diverse hires and monitoring the percentage of employees from different backgrounds is essential, it is the cultural changes that mark the true success of a DEI strategy. A thriving DEI environment is one where every individual—no matter their race, gender, age, or background—feels like they have an equal opportunity to succeed and thrive. This is where the work begins and where it needs to continue, even when the numbers are positive.

Creating a culture where individuals feel seen, heard, and respected is fundamental. People need to feel safe bringing their full selves to work, knowing they won't be judged or marginalized based on who they are. This doesn't just improve individual morale but also leads to increased creativity, innovation, and overall organizational success. This culture is nurtured over time with sustained commitment, education, and genuine leadership.

Engaging Your Teams: The Heart of DEI Success

True DEI success doesn't happen in isolation or from the top down—it's driven by engagement at all levels. From leadership to entry-level employees, creating an inclusive culture requires everyone to be on board and actively involved. Engaging teams in conversations about DEI, listening to their concerns, and making them part of the solution create a sense of shared ownership in the process.

An organization that fosters open dialogue and collaboration allows people to share their experiences, challenges, and ideas without fear of retaliation or judgment. This means holding spaces for employees to voice their opinions and having mechanisms in place to respond to those voices with respect and action.

Celebrating Wins: Big and Small

One of the most potent ways to keep momentum in a DEI initiative is by celebrating the wins, both big and small. Achieving a major milestone like the successful recruitment of a diverse leadership team is worth acknowledging. However, a small win like a team-building activity where employees share stories from their backgrounds or a department that implements unconscious bias training.

Celebrating these victories not only boosts morale but also demonstrates progress. It shows everyone involved that the effort is paying off and encourages people to stay committed to the journey. These celebrations should never feel like mere performances or tokenism—they should be heartfelt acknowledgements of the hard work and strides taken toward true inclusion.

Honesty in Addressing Gaps

One of the most critical steps in DEI success is addressing the gaps with honesty. No organization, no matter how committed, is perfect. There will always be areas that need improvement, and it's essential to acknowledge these gaps rather than shy away from them.

An organization's willingness to be transparent about where it's falling short is not a sign of failure; rather, it's a sign of growth. Openly admitting where progress is lacking and then developing actionable plans to address those shortcomings is the kind of accountability that fuels DEI's success. This also fosters trust within the organization, as employees see that their leaders are genuinely invested in continuous improvement and not merely putting up a facade.

What Gets Measured Gets Managed

As the saying goes, "What gets measured gets managed." This principle is fundamental when it comes to DEI. Setting clear, measurable goals helps an organization stay focused on the actions that will bring about real change. Metrics like diversity hiring statistics, employee retention rates, and internal promotions among underrepresented groups give insight into how well DEI initiatives are being implemented.

However, it's not just about tracking numbers for the sake of tracking numbers. Measuring brings attention to areas where improvement is necessary. It allows organizations to assess what is working and what isn't and make informed decisions about how to improve.

Meaningful Change Through Management

Once the goals are set and the gaps are identified, it's time to focus on management. The data gathered from measurements should not sit on a shelf or be locked away in a report. It must be used to inform strategies, design action plans, and influence decision-making. DEI management is about ensuring that resources, efforts, and programs align with the goal of creating a more inclusive and equitable environment.

When DEI is managed properly—when leadership, HR, and every team member actively work toward continuous improvement—it drives the kind of meaningful change that can reshape an organization. This change goes beyond the surface and cultivates a culture where every individual feels valued, included, and empowered to thrive.

In the end, measuring DEI success is about much more than just the numbers. It's about building a culture that fosters belonging, engagement, and accountability. It's about acknowledging achievements, addressing shortcomings honestly, and creating systems that manage meaningful change. What gets measured gets managed, and what gets managed is the engine that drives progress.

Let's be clear: DEI success is not a destination but a journey. By committing to continuous improvement, celebrating every step forward, and holding ourselves accountable, we can build workplaces where everyone is given the opportunity to be their best selves—free from bias and full of potential.

THE ROLE OF TECHNOLOGY IN DIVERSITY, EQUITY, AND INCLUSION (DEI)

In the evolving landscape of business and society, technology has emerged as a powerful tool that can drive progress toward diversity, equity, and inclusion (DEI). From artificial intelligence (AI) to data analytics, tech offers a range of opportunities to foster a more inclusive environment. However, like any tool, technology comes with its own set of challenges and responsibilities. In this article, we will explore two critical aspects of technology's role in DEI: AI and unconscious bias, and the ethical considerations in using tech to advance DEI efforts.

AI and Unconscious Bias

Artificial Intelligence (AI) has undeniably transformed numerous industries, from healthcare and finance to marketing and hiring practices. By automating repetitive tasks, streamlining complex processes, and analyzing large volumes of data, AI holds the promise of significantly improving efficiency, decision-making, and even predicting future trends. Its potential to enhance productivity and innovation is vast. However, as AI systems are designed and developed by humans, they are not immune to the biases and assumptions that we carry, often unconsciously, in our everyday lives. In fact, AI can unintentionally perpetuate or even amplify these biases if not carefully managed and monitored.

Unconscious bias refers to the prejudices or attitudes that we hold, often outside of our awareness, toward people based on factors such as race, gender, age, socioeconomic status, or other demographic characteristics. These biases influence our thoughts, behaviors, and decision-making processes, often without us realizing it. For instance, when we make decisions in hiring, promotions, or customer service, unconscious biases can shape our judgment and lead to unequal outcomes.

AI systems are particularly susceptible to these biases because they are typically trained on historical data sets. If the data used to train an AI model reflects past patterns of inequality or prejudice, the AI is likely to learn and reproduce those same biases in its outputs. For example, an AI-powered recruitment tool that analyzes historical hiring data may favor candidates who fit the profile of those traditionally hired in a particular role. If the data predominantly consists of male candidates for technical roles, the AI may inadvertently prioritize male candidates, perpetuating gender disparities in these fields.

This unintentional amplification of bias is not just an inconvenience; it can have serious consequences. In the context of hiring, for instance, biased AI tools could systematically disadvantage qualified candidates from underrepresented groups, reinforcing existing societal inequalities. Similarly, in areas like healthcare, biased algorithms could lead to unequal access to treatments or services for specific demographic groups, exacerbating health disparities. These biases undermine the fundamental goals of Diversity, Equity, and Inclusion (DEI), hindering efforts to create fair and inclusive environments.

The risks of AI amplifying unconscious bias are particularly concerning when these systems are used to make high-stakes decisions that can impact people's lives. For instance, if an AI system is used to assess job candidates, allocate promotions, or determine loan eligibility, biased outputs could limit opportunities for specific groups and reinforce systemic discrimination. Organizations must be vigilant in designing and implementing AI systems that promote fairness, transparency, and inclusivity.

To mitigate the risks of bias in AI, AI systems must undergo careful monitoring and adjustment throughout their lifecycle. One important strategy is diversifying the data used to train AI models. By ensuring that training data is representative of a broad range of perspectives and experiences, AI systems can better reflect the diversity of the populations they are intended to serve. In addition, ongoing auditing and testing of AI models for fairness are essential to identify and address any unintended biases that may arise over time. This requires collaboration between AI developers, DEI experts, and stakeholders from various demographic groups to ensure that AI systems operate fairly and equitably.

Furthermore, human oversight is key to minimizing the risk of bias. While AI can process large amounts of data and make decisions at incredible speed, human judgment is still crucial in interpreting the results and ensuring that decisions are made in accordance with DEI principles. By combining the power of AI with human expertise and ethical decision-making, we can create systems that support fairness and inclusion rather than perpetuate bias.

In conclusion, while AI offers immense potential for improving efficiency and innovation, it is essential to recognize and address the biases that may be embedded in these systems. By understanding the impact of unconscious bias in AI and taking proactive steps to mitigate its effects, we can ensure that technology serves as a force for good in promoting diversity, equity, and inclusion. In doing so, we can move closer to building a more just and equitable society, both in the workplace and beyond.

Ethical Considerations in Using Tech for DEI

While technology has immense potential to support DEI initiatives, its use must be guided by ethical principles to ensure it doesn't inadvertently perpetuate harm or injustice. Some key ethical considerations when leveraging technology for DEI include:

1. **Privacy and Data Security**:

Technology increasingly depends on the collection and analysis of vast amounts of data, including sensitive personal information. This data serves as the foundation for many modern technological tools, such as AI systems, data-driven decision-making processes, and predictive analytics. Within the realm of Diversity, Equity, and Inclusion (DEI), such data encompass demographic information, employee feedback, performance reviews, recruitment data, and engagement surveys. These data sets provide valuable insights that organizations can use to identify disparities, track progress, and design strategies to foster a more inclusive workplace.

However, the collection and use of sensitive personal data for DEI initiatives come with significant ethical and legal responsibilities. Organizations must maintain full transparency regarding how this data is collected, stored, processed, and utilized. Employees, customers, and other stakeholders must be informed about the purpose for which their data is being used, the specific types of data being collected, and how the information will be leveraged to promote DEI objectives.

Individuals must also be informed of their rights, including their ability to opt out, access, or request the deletion of their personal data. Transparent consent protocols are essential to ensuring that data collection is voluntary and informed. People should never feel coerced or misled into sharing personal information, and they should have the autonomy to decide how much information they wish to provide, especially when it involves sensitive personal characteristics such as race, gender, or sexual orientation.

Equally important is the protection of personal data against misuse or unauthorized access. With the rising threat of data breaches, organizations must implement robust data security measures, such as encryption, secure storage, and access controls. In addition, companies must regularly audit their data security practices to ensure they are up-to-date with evolving cybersecurity threats. Ethical use of data also means minimizing the amount of personal information collected to what is strictly necessary for achieving DEI goals, further reducing the risk of misuse.

Building and maintaining trust is central to the ethical use of data in DEI efforts. By demonstrating a commitment to transparency, obtaining explicit consent, and ensuring data security, organizations can foster a culture of accountability and respect. When individuals feel confident that their data is being handled responsibly, they are more likely to engage in

DEI initiatives and support organizational efforts to create a fairer and more inclusive environment. Ultimately, the ethical handling of data in DEI programs not only promotes compliance with legal requirements but also strengthens relationships with employees, customers, and other stakeholders.

2. **Transparency and Accountability**:

When technology, particularly AI, is used to make decisions that significantly impact people's lives—whether it's in hiring, promotions, resource allocation, or performance evaluations—it is essential to prioritize transparency in how these decisions are made. The integration of AI systems and data-driven models should not be a "black box" where the process and reasoning behind decisions remain hidden from employees or the public. For these technologies to be trusted and fair, the algorithms that power them must be explainable and understandable to all stakeholders, including employees, job candidates, customers, and even regulatory bodies.

Transparency in AI systems means that organizations should clearly articulate how and why a particular decision was made. For example, suppose an AI system is used to screen job applicants. In that case, organizations should be able to explain the specific factors or criteria the algorithm considered in making its recommendations or decisions. This allows both employees and the public to better understand the underlying logic and reasoning of the technology, ensuring that it aligns with ethical standards and does not unfairly disadvantage any particular group.

If AI or data-driven models lead to inequitable outcomes—such as favoring one group over another based on biased data or flawed algorithmic design—organizations must take accountability for these outcomes. Being transparent about mistakes, recognizing their impact, and addressing the underlying causes of bias or unfairness is crucial. This commitment to accountability requires organizations to be proactive in identifying and mitigating risks associated with biased algorithms. In cases where inequities are discovered, organizations must be willing to take immediate action, including revisiting their data, auditing their algorithms, and making necessary adjustments to improve fairness.

Moreover, organizations should develop mechanisms for feedback and redress. This means providing employees, customers, and other stakeholders with avenues to report perceived inequities or errors in AI decision-making. Such feedback should be taken seriously and incorporated into ongoing efforts to refine and improve AI systems. Regular audits, in which external experts assess the fairness and transparency of AI processes, should also be conducted to ensure that the technology continues to serve its intended purpose without reinforcing bias or inequality.

Ultimately, the goal is not just to prevent harm but to actively create a system where AI contributes positively to diversity, equity, and inclusion goals. When AI-driven decisions are made with transparency, accountability, and fairness in mind, they can become a powerful tool in advancing DEI efforts and promoting trust among all involved.

3. Bias in Algorithm Design

As mentioned, algorithms are not neutral—they can inherit biases from the data they are trained on. These biases may reflect historical inequalities or existing prejudices, which, if unchecked, can perpetuate harmful stereotypes and reinforce societal disparities.

The ethical use of technology requires a steadfast commitment to ensuring that algorithms are designed to be fair, equitable, and transparent. This commitment must go beyond merely detecting bias; it involves building an inclusive framework that actively mitigates bias and promotes diversity at every stage of the algorithm's development.

One key aspect of ensuring fairness is assembling **diverse teams of developers**. A diverse team brings a wide range of perspectives, backgrounds, and life experiences to the table, which helps to identify and address potential blind spots that a more homogenous team might miss. For example, developers from different ethnic backgrounds, genders, and socioeconomic statuses may recognize biases in algorithms that affect their communities, prompting adjustments that might otherwise be overlooked.

Moreover, it is critical to **engage with marginalized communities during the design and development process**. Those who are most likely to be impacted by biased technology—such as people of color, women, or individuals from lower-income backgrounds—should have a voice in shaping the technology they interact with. This can involve conducting focus groups, gathering feedback, or even involving representatives of marginalized groups in the design and testing phases. By listening to those who are often excluded or misrepresented, we can better understand the nuances of bias and create technology that truly serves everyone.

Another crucial element of creating fair algorithms is **actively working to identify and address biases before they reach users**. Bias detection should not be a one-time task but an ongoing process. Regular audits, both internal and external, should be conducted to assess the fairness of algorithms and identify potential disparities in outcomes. This requires leveraging a combination of testing, data analysis, and machine learning techniques that evaluate whether the algorithm treats all individuals fairly, regardless of their background or characteristics. If bias is detected, developers must be prepared to revise the algorithm and retrain it using more representative, unbiased data.

Without these proactive measures, technology could inadvertently reinforce existing disparities rather than challenge them. For instance, in recruitment, biased algorithms might perpetuate the underrepresentation of certain groups in specific industries by favoring candidates from backgrounds that align with historically dominant demographics. In healthcare, biased algorithms may prioritize treatment for certain conditions more common in one demographic, leading to unequal access to care. The consequences of such biased decisions are far-reaching, affecting not only individuals but entire communities.

Ultimately, creating fair and unbiased algorithms is not just about fixing problems as they arise—it's about fostering a culture of ethical responsibility and inclusivity from the outset. When technology is designed with fairness and equity in mind, it has the potential to be a powerful force for good, challenging inequality and creating opportunities for all, regardless of their background.

4. Equitable Access

The rapid pace of technological advancement presents both opportunities and challenges in the pursuit of diversity, equity, and inclusion (DEI). One of the most pressing concerns is that not everyone has equal access to the tools, training, and opportunities necessary to benefit from these innovations. As technology continues to evolve, a digital divide emerges, which can disproportionately affect certain groups, particularly those from lower socioeconomic backgrounds or marginalized communities.

For organizations to indeed promote DEI through technology, they must ensure all employees, regardless of their financial status, geographic location, or technological literacy, can equally access and leverage these tools. This involves a thoughtful approach to how technologies are implemented, used, and integrated into the workplace. If not carefully managed, the very tools that are designed to promote fairness and inclusion could unintentionally widen existing gaps, further alienating those already at a disadvantage.

To level the playing field, organizations must consider several strategies:

1. **Investing in Training and Skill Development**: A key component of ensuring equitable access is providing employees with the knowledge and skills needed to effectively use new technologies. This may require offering targeted training programs that cater to different learning styles, levels of prior

knowledge, and specific needs. For example, introductory digital literacy courses can be offered to individuals who are less familiar with technology. At the same time, more advanced training can be available for those seeking to deepen their expertise. Organizations can also create mentorship programs that pair tech-savvy employees with those who may need extra support, ensuring that no one is left behind as they integrate new tools.

2. **Providing Tech Resources to Underrepresented Groups**: Not every employee may have access to the latest devices, high-speed internet, or software necessary to engage with cutting-edge technology. Companies should consider providing necessary resources to underrepresented groups within the organization to bridge this gap. This could include providing laptops or tablets, offering stipends for internet services, or supplying specialized tools and software required for specific roles. By removing technological barriers, organizations empower employees

from all backgrounds to participate fully in the digital transformation.

3. **Tailoring Technology to Diverse Needs**: Technological tools must be designed with accessibility in mind. Many employees face challenges related to disabilities or different learning needs, and organizations must ensure the technologies they use are inclusive. This can involve ensuring that platforms are compatible with screen readers, offering speech-to-text features, or providing customizable user interfaces that allow employees to adjust settings based on their preferences. When technology is adaptable and mindful of diverse needs, it ensures that all employees have an equal opportunity to succeed.

4. **Promoting Digital Inclusion through Policy**: Beyond individual training efforts and resource allocation, organizations can promote digital inclusion by implementing company-wide policies focused on accessibility. This includes setting clear goals for digital equity, regularly auditing technology platforms for inclusivity, and ensuring that DEI initiatives

include a specific focus on digital inclusion. It's also essential for organizations to foster an inclusive culture where employees feel comfortable expressing any difficulties they face with technology and can seek assistance without fear of judgment.

5. **Fostering a Culture of Continuous Learning**: As technology evolves, the need for ongoing education and adaptation is essential. Organizations can support DEI by cultivating a culture of continuous learning, where employees at all levels are encouraged to keep developing their technological proficiency. This can be achieved through regular workshops, webinars, or online courses that are accessible to everyone in the company. Additionally, companies should encourage employees to stay informed about new developments in technology that could enhance their work and ensure that training is not seen as a one-time event but as an ongoing process that evolves with the technology.

By ensuring equitable access to technology, organizations can create a more inclusive environment where every employee, regardless of their background or technical expertise, has the tools and knowledge necessary to succeed. It's not enough to introduce new technologies into the workplace; organizations must actively work to remove barriers to access and ensure that these tools are truly accessible to all. This investment in training, resources, and inclusive practices is not only beneficial to individual employees but is a critical component of creating a truly diverse, equitable, and inclusive workplace. Through these efforts, companies can ensure that technology becomes a catalyst for DEI, empowering employees from all walks of life to thrive in the digital age.

The Future of Tech-Driven DEI

Technology holds immense potential to accelerate Diversity, Equity, and Inclusion (DEI) efforts, offering organizations innovative tools to identify disparities, track progress, and build more inclusive environments. From AI-powered analytics to data-driven insights, technology enables businesses to monitor and address DEI gaps more efficiently than ever before. However, as with any technological advancement, the use of these tools must be approached with careful consideration and ethical responsibility.

One of the most significant opportunities technology offers is the ability to objectively measure and analyze DEI metrics across organizations. By using data to assess hiring practices, employee performance, pay equity, and workplace culture, businesses can gain a clearer understanding of where inequalities exist and how to address them. This level of insight helps organizations make informed decisions that drive meaningful change, allowing them to track their progress over time and ensure their DEI initiatives are genuinely effective.

However, the integration of technology into DEI strategies comes with its own set of challenges, especially when it comes to the use of artificial intelligence (AI). AI has the potential to revolutionize the way we make decisions, but it also poses a risk if not carefully managed. AI systems, particularly those used in recruitment, hiring, and promotions, can inherit biases from historical data, leading to outcomes that unintentionally perpetuate inequality. These biases often arise from unconscious prejudices embedded in past decisions, which AI models may replicate if they are trained on biased datasets.

To fully realize AI's benefits in DEI, it is crucial to actively address unconscious bias in algorithms and ensure that AI tools are designed with fairness in mind. This includes diversifying training data, regularly auditing AI models for bias, and implementing checks and balances to ensure that human judgment is part of the decision-making process. AI should complement human oversight, not replace it, ensuring that decisions made by technology are aligned with the values of inclusion and fairness.

Another key ethical consideration is the responsible use of data. Technology relies on collecting and analyzing vast amounts of information, and this data often includes sensitive personal details, such as race, gender, disability status, and other demographic factors. While this data can be valuable in identifying disparities and improving DEI practices, it also raises concerns about privacy, security, and potential misuse. Organizations must be transparent about how data is collected, stored, and used, and they must establish strong safeguards to protect individuals' privacy. Clear consent procedures, along with robust data security measures, are necessary to build trust and ensure that data is used in a way that respects individuals' rights.

Moreover, technology must be accessible to all employees, regardless of their background or technological expertise. As digital tools become more embedded in the workplace, it is essential to ensure that these tools do not create new barriers for marginalized groups. Providing training and resources for employees, particularly those from underrepresented communities, ensures that everyone can fully participate in DEI initiatives. This commitment to equitable access empowers individuals and strengthens the organization's overall diversity and inclusion efforts.

The future of DEI-driven technology is exciting, but it also requires careful stewardship. To harness the full potential of technology in promoting diversity, equity, and inclusion, we must strike a balance between innovation and ethical responsibility. As organizations continue to adopt new technologies, they must remain vigilant in addressing issues like unconscious bias, data privacy, and accessibility. By prioritizing human values and ensuring that technology is used with a clear ethical framework, we can create a more diverse, equitable, and inclusive world. The role of technology in DEI is not just about implementing new tools—it's about using those tools to uphold the values of fairness, respect, and equality that are the foundation of any inclusive society.

SUSTAINING CHANGE

In modern times, maintaining change is no longer an option—it's required. Businesses that fail to adapt risk falling behind in a more competitive landscape. However, embracing change is only the first step. To fully sustain it, firms must incorporate accountability into their working procedures while being adaptable to a changing workforce. Here's how to make it happen!

Building Accountability into Workplace Practices

Accountability isn't about pointing fingers; it's about ownership, trust, and commitment. When employees take responsibility for their roles and contributions, change becomes a shared journey rather than a top-down directive. But how do you foster accountability?

1. **Clear Expectations**

Ambiguity is the enemy of accountability—it creates confusion, stalls progress, and allows missed opportunities. To build a culture of accountability, organizations must prioritize clarity in every aspect of their operations. This starts with clearly defining goals, roles, and responsibilities.

When team members clearly understand their purpose and the specific outcomes expected of them, they can focus their efforts more effectively. Instead of second-guessing their next steps or wasting time deciphering vague instructions, they can channel their energy into meaningful contributions. Clarity also eliminates overlaps and gaps in responsibilities, ensuring that no task is left undone or duplicated.

For instance, a well-defined goal might include not just *what* needs to be achieved but also the *why*, *how*, and *when*. Providing measurable objectives, timelines, and actionable steps empowers employees to take ownership of their work. This fosters confidence and autonomy, allowing individuals to make decisions within their scope without constant oversight.

Moreover, clarity goes beyond individual tasks; it should extend to team dynamics. Clearly outlining how different roles interconnect and contribute to the larger organizational mission fosters collaboration and mutual accountability. Each member understands not just their role but also how their efforts impact the team's success.

In practice, this might involve creating a shared document or project roadmap that outlines deliverables, deadlines, and responsible parties. Leaders can also hold kickoff meetings to align expectations and provide opportunities for team members to ask questions or seek clarification. By eliminating ambiguity, organizations create a foundation where accountability thrives, and employees are equipped to excel.

2. **Regular Feedback**

Annual reviews have their place, but relying on them as the sole touchpoint for discussing progress is outdated and ineffective. Change happens quickly, and waiting months to address issues or recognize achievements can stall momentum. Instead, regular check-ins create a dynamic feedback loop that keeps teams aligned, motivated, and on track toward their goals.

Frequent check-ins serve multiple purposes. They provide an opportunity to **course-correct** when things veer off track, ensuring that minor missteps don't evolve into more significant setbacks. Teams can identify and address challenges early, whether it's a resource gap, miscommunication, or shifting priorities. This proactive approach saves time and builds trust by showing employees that their efforts are being monitored and supported in real-time.

Beyond solving problems, regular check-ins also offer a platform to **celebrate wins**—no matter how small. Acknowledging achievements as they happen reinforces positive behaviors, boosts morale, and strengthens the bond between team members and leadership. Celebrating progress doesn't have to be elaborate; even a simple "great job" during a meeting can go a long way in making employees feel valued.

However, the cornerstone of these interactions is **constructive feedback**. Feedback should be specific, actionable, and focused on growth. Instead of framing conversations around what went wrong, emphasize what can be improved and how. For instance, instead of saying, "You missed the deadline," a more constructive approach might be, "Let's explore what caused the delay and how we can adjust timelines or support you better for future projects." This not only addresses the issue but also empowers the employee to improve without feeling punished.

To make regular check-ins effective, organizations should create a structured yet flexible process. This could involve weekly one-on-one meetings, bi-weekly team reviews, or monthly performance snapshots, depending on the team's needs. Digital tools like project management software or performance-tracking apps can facilitate these discussions, making it easier to document progress and revisit key points later.

Ultimately, the goal of regular check-ins is to foster a culture of continuous improvement, open communication, and mutual support. When done right, they become not just a management tool but a meaningful way to build stronger, more engaged teams.

3. Lead by Example

Accountability is a cultural cornerstone that begins at the top. Leaders set the tone for how accountability is perceived, embraced, and practiced within an organization. When leaders model the behaviors they expect from their teams, they foster an environment of trust, respect, and mutual responsibility. Simply put, accountability cascades from the top down.

To lead by example, leaders must first **demonstrate transparency**. This means openly admitting mistakes, owning up to decisions—both good and bad—and taking responsibility for outcomes. Far from being a sign of weakness, this level of honesty humanizes leaders and builds credibility. When employees see their leaders take ownership, they are more likely to do the same, knowing that accountability isn't about blame but about growth and integrity.

For instance, if a project misses its mark, a strong leader doesn't deflect the blame onto their team. Instead, they might say, "I take responsibility for not clarifying the goals or providing enough resources. Let's discuss how we can prevent this in the future." This approach not only sets a powerful example but also creates a safe space for open dialogue and collective problem-solving.

Moreover, leaders must embody **consistency in their actions and expectations**. Holding themselves to the same, if not higher, standards as their team members reinforces fairness and accountability as core values. A leader who demands punctuality but regularly shows up late to meetings undermines their credibility. On the other hand, a leader who consistently meets deadlines fulfills promises and acknowledges their own areas for improvement inspires others to follow suit.

Another critical aspect is recognizing that accountability is a **two-way street**. Leaders should not only expect accountability from their teams but also welcome it in return. Encouraging employees to provide feedback or challenge decisions when appropriate demonstrates humility and openness. For example, a leader might say, "If you think there's a better way to approach this, I'd love to hear your thoughts." This approach strengthens collaboration and reinforces the idea that accountability is a shared responsibility.

Leaders can further embed accountability into their teams by implementing systems that support it, such as regular performance reviews, transparent goal-setting processes, and mechanisms for tracking progress. However, these systems must be underpinned by a culture where accountability is seen as empowering rather than punitive.

Ultimately, when leaders walk the talk, they inspire confidence and foster a culture where accountability becomes second nature. By admitting their own missteps, owning their decisions, and inviting constructive dialogue, leaders demonstrate that accountability is not just a principle—it's a practice that drives success for the entire organization.

4. **Empower Decision-Making**

Micromanaging frustrates employees more than frustrates them—it stifles creativity, undermines confidence, and erodes accountability. Leaders who micromanage inadvertently send the message that they don't trust their team's abilities, which can lead to disengagement and a "check-the-box" mentality. In contrast, empowering employees to make decisions within their roles fosters ownership, innovation, and a stronger commitment to organizational goals.

Empowerment starts with trust. By giving employees, the autonomy to make decisions and take initiative, leaders show that they value their team's expertise and judgment. This trust acts as a catalyst for accountability, as employees are more likely to take ownership of their tasks when they feel empowered to shape the outcomes. When people are trusted to lead their projects, they move beyond merely completing assignments—they become active contributors to the organization's success.

For example, consider a manager overseeing a product launch. Instead of dictating every step, they might outline the overall objectives and let their team develop the strategy. This approach allows team members to leverage their unique skills and perspectives, fostering creativity and engagement. If challenges arise, employees are more likely to proactively address them, knowing they have the authority and responsibility to act.

To effectively empower employees, leaders must ensure they have the right resources, support, and clear guidelines. Autonomy doesn't mean leaving employees to fend for themselves—it's about striking a balance between guidance and freedom. Leaders can achieve this by setting clear expectations, providing the necessary tools and training, and offering regular support without overstepping boundaries.

Empowerment also drives sustained engagement with change. When employees have a hand in decision-making, they are more likely to embrace change because they feel a sense of ownership over the process.

For instance, during organizational transitions, involving employees in discussions about new processes or tools ensures they feel invested in the outcome. This not only smooths the transition but also helps embed lasting change.

In essence, empowerment is about shifting the mindset from control to collaboration. Leaders who empower their teams don't just delegate tasks—they build trust, encourage innovation, and create a culture where accountability thrives naturally. When employees feel trusted and valued, they rise to the occasion, taking pride in their work and driving meaningful, sustained change within the organization.

5. Celebrate Successes

Recognizing and rewarding individuals and teams who demonstrate accountability is an essential step in building a strong, values-driven workplace culture. When employees see that their efforts to take ownership, make responsible decisions, and contribute meaningfully are noticed and appreciated, it reinforces the importance of accountability as a core principle. This recognition not only validates their hard work but also inspires others to adopt the same mindset, creating a positive ripple effect throughout the organization.

Public acknowledgment is a powerful tool in fostering accountability. When leaders share stories of employees or teams who have gone above and beyond, it shines a spotlight on the kind of behavior the organization values. Whether it's during a meeting, in an internal communication, or at a company event, celebrating these moments sends a clear message: accountability matters, and it's worth celebrating.

Equally impactful is the personal touch of recognition. A sincere thank-you from a leader, a note of appreciation, or even a meaningful conversation acknowledging someone's efforts can leave a lasting impression. These moments show employees that their contributions are not only noticed but also deeply valued, creating a sense of pride and belonging.

Rewarding accountability can also take many forms. While monetary incentives or tangible rewards like gift cards and professional development opportunities are compelling, sometimes the reward lies in simple yet meaningful gestures. Giving employees a platform to share their achievements, such as presenting their work or leading a project, can be incredibly motivating. Recognizing accountability doesn't just highlight success; it underscores the importance of learning from challenges, demonstrating that taking ownership—even when things don't go as planned—is equally commendable.

Celebrating accountability fosters an environment where trust and mutual respect thrive. When teams feel their efforts are appreciated, they're more likely to embrace responsibility, collaborate effectively, and innovate. Over time, this culture of recognition builds a workplace where accountability isn't just a principle but a shared practice, deeply woven into the fabric of the organization.

Organizations foster a community of engaged, empowered, and high-performing individuals by recognizing and celebrating those who demonstrate accountability, resulting in overall success.

In reality, this could look like weekly team meetings when each member presents their progress, challenges, and future steps. Alternatively, it could entail deploying tools such as project management software to keep everyone on the same page. Regardless of the approach, the goal is to create an environment in which accountability is embedded in the fabric of the workplace.

Adapting to a Changing Workforce

The workforce is not what it used to be—and that's a good thing. With generational shifts, technological advancements, and increasing diversity, the modern workplace is a melting pot of skills, experiences, and expectations. Sustaining change means adapting to these dynamics.

1. **Understand Generational Needs**

The modern workplace is a rich tapestry of generations, each bringing unique strengths, perspectives, and preferences. From Baby Boomers and Gen X to Millennials and Gen Z, these diverse cohorts contribute to a dynamic and innovative environment. However, sustaining harmony and fostering collaboration across these generational lines requires intentional effort and understanding.

Baby Boomers, often characterized by their strong work ethic and loyalty, tend to value structure, stability, and clear hierarchies. They appreciate well-defined roles and processes, as these provide a sense of reliability and predictability in the workplace. Their extensive experience often makes them excellent mentors and leaders who can guide younger generations through challenges.

Gen X, known as the "bridge generation," brings a pragmatic and independent approach to work. They often value autonomy and efficiency, making them adept at balancing traditional and modern workplace practices. Their adaptability allows them to connect with both older and younger colleagues, fostering collaboration across generational divides.

Millennials, who grew up during the digital revolution, often prioritize flexibility, purpose, and meaningful work. They thrive in environments that offer opportunities for growth, creativity, and work-life balance. Millennials also value feedback and recognition, as these reinforce their sense of contribution and engagement.

Gen Z, the newest entrants into the workforce, are digital natives with a strong inclination toward innovation and diversity. They seek workplaces that align with their personal values, such as sustainability, inclusivity, and social responsibility. They are highly collaborative but also value independence, often looking for roles that allow them to learn quickly and make an immediate impact.

To build a workplace that capitalizes on these generational strengths, it's essential to **create a balance that respects their differences while encouraging mutual understanding**. For example:

- **Flexible Work Models**: While Baby Boomers and Gen X may prefer traditional office setups, Millennials and Gen Z often seek remote or hybrid options. Offering flexibility accommodates these preferences without compromising productivity.

- **Purpose-Driven Initiatives**: Millennials and Gen Z are drawn to organizations with clear missions and values. By embedding purpose into the company culture, businesses can engage these employees while also inspiring Baby Boomers and Gen X to connect with the broader vision.

- **Cross-Generational Mentorship**: Pairing Baby Boomers and Gen X with Millennials and

Gen Z fosters knowledge sharing. While older employees can impart wisdom and experience, younger employees can offer fresh perspectives and technological insights.

- **Customized Communication**: Generations often prefer different modes of communication. Baby Boomers and Gen X may lean toward in-person or email interactions, while Millennials and Gen Z often prefer instant messaging or video calls. Adapting communication styles ensures everyone feels heard and included.

- **Inclusive Decision-Making**: Involving representatives from all generations in decision-making processes promotes buy-in and ensures diverse perspectives are considered. This leads to more innovative and well-rounded solutions.

When organizations recognize and embrace each generation's unique contributions, they create an environment where everyone feels valued and empowered. By fostering collaboration, encouraging open dialogue, and thoughtfully addressing generational needs, businesses can transform their workforce into a cohesive team that drives sustained success and innovation.

2. Embrace Technology

Remote work, artificial intelligence (AI), and advanced collaboration tools have revolutionized the way businesses operate, making flexibility and innovation essential for success. These technological advancements are no longer optional—they're the backbone of modern workplaces. To stay competitive and sustain change, organizations must not only invest in cutting-edge technology but also ensure that employees are equipped to harness their full potential effectively.

The New Age of Work

Remote work has redefined traditional office dynamics. No longer tethered to a single location, teams can collaborate across time zones, bringing together diverse perspectives and skills. Similarly, AI is transforming workflows by automating repetitive tasks, analyzing vast amounts of data in seconds, and offering predictive insights that were once impossible to achieve manually. Collaboration tools, such as project management platforms, video conferencing apps, and cloud-based storage solutions, bridge the gap between remote and on-site teams, enabling seamless communication and productivity.

The Importance of Investing in the Right Technology

However, adopting technology isn't just about choosing the latest tools. It's about selecting the right solutions tailored to your organization's unique needs. For instance, a creative agency might benefit from design-centric collaboration platforms, while a tech firm may need advanced analytics tools powered by AI. Conducting a needs assessment ensures that the chosen technology aligns with your goals and workflows rather than introducing unnecessary complexity.

Equally important is scalability. As businesses grow, their technological needs evolve. Investing in tools that can scale alongside the organization prevents the disruption of frequent platform overhauls. Additionally, prioritizing user-friendly interfaces reduces learning curves, enabling teams to integrate new tools into their routines seamlessly.

Empowering Employees Through Training

Technology is only as effective as the people using it. Comprehensive training ensures employees are confident and proficient with the tools at their disposal. This goes beyond introductory tutorials—training should be ongoing, covering updates, best practices, and advanced features that enhance efficiency. For example, hosting regular workshops or offering access to online learning resources can keep teams up to speed with technological advancements.

Moreover, involving employees in the decision-making process when selecting new tools can boost buy-in and engagement. When employees feel their input is valued, they are more likely to embrace and effectively utilize new technologies.

Technology as an Enabler, Not a Burden

The ultimate goal of technology should be to enhance work, not complicate it. Tools should simplify processes, improve communication, and save time. If a piece of technology creates confusion, adds redundant steps, or overwhelms employees, it may be doing more harm than good. Regular feedback loops can help identify tools that need to be adjusted or replaced to better serve the organization's needs.

For instance, a streamlined project management tool that integrates seamlessly with email and file-sharing platforms can drastically reduce the time spent switching between apps. Similarly, AI-driven customer support systems can handle routine inquiries, allowing human agents to focus on more complex tasks.

The intersection of remote work, AI, and collaboration tools presents unparalleled opportunities for organizations to innovate and thrive. By strategically investing in the right technology and empowering employees with the skills to use it effectively, businesses can create an environment where technology serves as a powerful enabler rather than an obstacle. In this digital age, success isn't just about keeping up with change—it's about leading the charge.

3. Promote Diversity and Inclusion

A diverse workforce is more than a metric to meet or a box to tick—it's a decisive business advantage that can drive innovation, enhance decision-making, and strengthen organizational resilience. When individuals from different backgrounds, experiences, and perspectives come together, they bring fresh ideas and unique approaches to problem-solving, which can lead to transformative outcomes.

Diversity fuels creativity. Teams composed of people with varied cultural, educational, and professional experiences are more likely to challenge conventional thinking and explore new possibilities. For instance, a marketing campaign developed by a multicultural team is more likely to resonate with a broader audience as it incorporates insights that reflect a wide range of perspectives.

But diversity alone isn't enough; inclusion is the catalyst that unlocks its full potential. Without an inclusive environment, diverse voices can go unheard, and their contributions may be undervalued. This is why organizations must **invest in inclusion initiatives** that create a culture where every individual feels respected, supported, and empowered to contribute.

- **Establish Inclusive Policies:** Start with the foundation—clear, inclusive policies that ensure fairness in hiring, promotions, and workplace conduct. These policies should actively discourage discrimination and bias while promoting equal opportunities for all.

- **Encourage Open Dialogue:** Create safe spaces for employees to share their experiences and perspectives. Regular town halls, feedback sessions, or diversity councils can give employees a platform to voice their ideas and concerns, fostering a culture of mutual respect and understanding.

- **Provide Training and Education:** Offer diversity, equity, and inclusion (DEI) training to help employees and leaders recognize unconscious biases and develop strategies to overcome them. Training should go beyond awareness and provide actionable steps for building an inclusive workplace.

- **Celebrate Differences:** Acknowledge and celebrate cultural events, traditions, and milestones that are meaningful to your workforce. This not only shows that the organization values diversity but also helps build stronger connections among team members.

- **Hold Leadership Accountable:** Leaders play a pivotal role in shaping workplace culture. Make inclusion a leadership priority by setting measurable goals and holding leaders accountable for fostering an inclusive environment.

By ensuring that **every voice is heard and valued**, organizations can tap into their teams' collective intelligence, leading to better decisions and stronger business outcomes. Research consistently shows that companies with diverse and inclusive workforces are more likely to outperform their peers financially, innovate faster, and attract top talent.

Inclusion isn't just good for business—it's the right thing to do. By embracing and investing in diversity and inclusion, organizations not only position themselves for success but also contribute to creating a more equitable and inclusive world.

4. Offer Growth Opportunities

Today's employees are looking for more than just a steady paycheck—they want growth, purpose, and opportunities to advance both personally and professionally. In an era where job satisfaction is closely tied to development opportunities, organizations that prioritize employee growth are better positioned to attract and retain top talent while fostering an engaged, future-ready workforce.

One of the most impactful ways to support employee development is through **mentorship programs**. Mentorship offers a dual benefit: seasoned professionals can pass on their expertise, while mentees gain valuable guidance to navigate challenges and achieve their career goals. A well-structured mentorship program not only enhances skills but also builds meaningful relationships within the organization, creating a sense of community and belonging. This is especially crucial in larger or hybrid workplaces where employees may otherwise feel disconnected.

In addition to mentorship, investing in **upskilling and reskilling programs** is essential in today's fast-evolving job market. With advancements in technology and shifting industry demands, employees need to continuously adapt their skills to remain relevant. Organizations can offer training programs, workshops, or access to online learning platforms that allow employees to grow their expertise in areas like digital tools, leadership, or emerging trends. By fostering a culture of learning, companies not only prepare their teams for future challenges but also demonstrate a commitment to their professional success.

Clear and attainable **career paths** are another key component of retaining and engaging talent. Employees want to see a future for themselves within the organization—whether that means climbing the leadership ladder, transitioning to new roles, or deepening their expertise in a specific field. Regular career development discussions, personalized growth plans, and opportunities for internal mobility help employees visualize their trajectory and stay motivated to achieve it.

For example, an employee might join as a junior analyst but aspire to become a team lead or subject matter expert. By providing a roadmap that includes necessary milestones—such as additional training, leadership workshops, or hands-on projects—the organization empowers them to take proactive steps toward their goal. This approach not only benefits the employee but also reduces turnover and strengthens the company's internal talent pipeline.

Lastly, development efforts should align with employees' intrinsic motivators. Beyond skills and promotions, employees often seek a sense of purpose in their work. Incorporating opportunities for them to contribute to meaningful projects, innovate, or take ownership of initiatives can ignite their passion and drive.

By creating an environment where mentorship, skill-building, and clear advancement opportunities are the norm, organizations can ensure their employees feel valued, challenged, and inspired. The result is a workplace culture that not only adapts to change but thrives in it, driven by an engaged, empowered, and eager-to-contribute team.

5. **Stay Agile**

Change is one of the few constants in life, and in the fast-paced world of work, the ability to pivot is not just beneficial—it's essential for survival and growth. Organizations that fail to adapt to risk stagnation, while those that embrace change position themselves for innovation and long-term success. To thrive in an ever-shifting landscape, businesses must cultivate a culture of adaptability where experimentation is welcomed and setbacks are reframed as valuable learning opportunities.

Encourage Experimentation

Innovation rarely happens without risk, and experimentation is the lifeblood of progress. When employees feel empowered to try new approaches and propose fresh ideas, they contribute to an agile, forward-thinking organization. Leaders can foster this environment by creating safe spaces where team members are encouraged to explore creative solutions without fear of failure. For example, introducing pilot projects or innovation workshops allows teams to test concepts on a smaller scale before full implementation.

However, encouraging experimentation also requires resources and support. Employees need access to the tools, training, and time necessary to think outside the box. Leaders should actively celebrate initiative and curiosity, reinforcing the idea that bold thinking is not only accepted but valued.

Reframe Setbacks as Learning Opportunities

In an adaptable culture, setbacks are not viewed as dead ends but as stepping stones toward improvement. Mistakes and missteps are inevitable in the pursuit of growth, but their impact depends on how they are handled. When organizations treat failures as learning experiences, they foster resilience and continuous improvement.

For instance, after a failed project, a team might conduct a retrospective meeting to analyze what went wrong, what could have been done differently, and what lessons can be applied moving forward. This approach normalizes the idea that setbacks are part of the journey and ensures the organization is better prepared for future challenges.

Build Flexibility into Processes

Adaptability is not just a mindset; it must also be woven into the organization's processes. Agile methodologies, for example, emphasize iterative development and regular reassessment, making it easier to adjust to changing circumstances. Similarly, creating flexible workflows and cross functional teams can enhance an organization's ability to pivot quickly when priorities shift.

Empower Employees to Embrace Change

An adaptable culture relies on employees who are open to learning and growth. Providing opportunities for professional development, upskilling, and cross-training helps employees feel confident in navigating new roles or technologies. When employees see change as an opportunity to expand their skills rather than a threat to their stability, they are more likely to embrace it enthusiastically.

Lead with Agility

Leadership plays a critical role in fostering adaptability. Leaders who model flexibility and a solutions-oriented mindset inspire their teams to do the same. By staying calm under pressure, openly communicating about changes, and demonstrating a willingness to pivot when necessary, leaders reinforce the importance of adaptability as a shared value.

Building a culture of adaptability isn't about eliminating challenges—it's about equipping teams to face them with creativity, resilience, and confidence. By encouraging experimentation, reframing setbacks as opportunities, and fostering a flexible mindset, organizations can transform change from a disruptive force into a powerful catalyst for growth and success. After all, in a world where the only certainty is change, adaptability is the ultimate competitive advantage.

For example, consider a company transitioning to hybrid work. Success lies in offering flexible schedules, equipping employees with the right tools, and fostering communication channels that bridge the gap between remote and on-site staff. Regular surveys can also provide insights into how employees feel about the changes and what adjustments might be needed.

Sustaining change is not a one-and-done effort—it's a dynamic, ongoing process that demands intentionality, resilience, and adaptability at every level of an organization. Change, by its very nature, is continuous, and thriving in this ever-evolving landscape requires more than initial enthusiasm. It calls for a strategic approach that embeds the ability to adapt into the very DNA of the organization.

A key component of sustaining change is **building accountability into workplace practices**. When accountability becomes a foundational principle, every team member understands their role in driving and maintaining progress. It fosters a sense of ownership and collective responsibility, ensuring that change is not seen as an external force but as a shared mission. Clear goals, regular feedback, and transparent communication create a framework where accountability thrives, empowering individuals and teams to consistently align their efforts with organizational objectives.

Equally important is the ability to **embrace the evolving needs of a diverse and dynamic workforce**. Today's workplace is characterized by rapid technological advancements, generational shifts, and increasing diversity. Organizations that sustain change recognize the value of adapting to these transformations, leveraging them as opportunities for growth and innovation. By promoting inclusivity, fostering continuous learning, and staying agile, businesses can turn workforce diversity into a competitive advantage.

Sustaining change also requires a **shift in mindset**. Rather than seeing change as a disruption to be managed, organizations must view it as a catalyst for improvement. This involves cultivating a culture where experimentation is encouraged, setbacks are treated as learning opportunities, and success is celebrated, no matter how small. When change is welcomed as a driver of growth, it becomes a strength rather than a challenge.

Ultimately, the ability to sustain change hinges on a commitment to evolution. Organizations that are intentional in their actions, resilient in the face of setbacks, and adaptable to new realities are those that not only survive but thrive. After all, the only constant in life and business is change itself—so why not embrace it, harness its potential, and make it your most significant competitive advantage?

PART V: BUILDING LONG-TERM COMMITMENT TO DIVERSITY AND INCLUSION

EMBEDDING BIAS REDUCTION INTO ORGANIZATIONAL STRATEGY

Creating a workplace that values diversity, equity, and inclusion (DEI) is neither a one-time endeavor or a collection of short-term projects. It is a long-term commitment that should be strongly ingrained in the organization's culture. To have a long-term influence, DEI must be integrated into the basic beliefs, strategic objectives, and operational practices of the firm.

Aligning Diversity Goals with Business Objectives

To be fully effective, DEI must be addressed as a strategic priority that is aligned with the organization's overall business objectives. If diversity efforts are perceived to be independent or unconnected from the company's vision, they are less likely to gain traction or have a meaningful impact. Here's how to align diversity goals and business objectives:

1. **Integrate DEI into the Mission and Vision**

Every company has a mission and vision that serve as the cornerstone of its strategy. These guiding statements outline the company's purpose, values, and aspirations, influencing every decision and action taken. However, in today's rapidly changing business environment, merely having a mission or vision is no longer enough. To create a truly inclusive and equitable workplace, diversity, equity, and inclusion (DEI) must be explicitly woven into these foundational documents.

By integrating DEI goals into the company's mission and vision, organizations not only demonstrate their commitment to these values but also set a clear direction for how diversity and inclusion will drive their success. This approach ensures that DEI is not viewed as an afterthought or an isolated initiative but rather as a core principle that aligns with and supports the broader organizational goals.

For instance, a company could state in its mission, "We are committed to creating an inclusive environment where diverse voices are heard, valued, and respected, fostering innovation and driving our business forward." This commitment sets the tone for how the company will operate, making it clear that diversity and inclusion are integral to its success and future growth.

Why This Matters

Embedding DEI into the mission and vision ensures that these values are present in every aspect of the business. It sends a strong signal to employees, customers, and partners that the organization is serious about diversity and is prepared to put in the work to make it a reality. Moreover, by aligning DEI goals with the company's strategic priorities, businesses can tap into the wealth of benefits that come from a diverse and inclusive workforce:

- **Innovation and Creativity**: A commitment to diversity and inclusion helps bring together people from different backgrounds, perspectives, and experiences. This diversity fosters creativity, leading to new ideas, solutions, and innovations that can give the company a competitive edge. When diverse voices are actively included in decision-making processes, the organization benefits from a broader range of ideas and solutions that cater to a wider customer base.

- **Employee Engagement and Retention**: Employees are more likely to feel valued and motivated when they work in an environment that respects and celebrates diversity. A company that embeds DEI into its mission and vision sends the message that it is dedicated to creating a supportive and welcoming workplace for all. This sense of belonging boosts employee morale, increases job satisfaction, and leads to higher retention rates.

- **Attracting Top Talent**: In today's talent-driven market, many job seekers prioritize working for companies that align with their values, including diversity and inclusion. By clearly stating DEI goals in the company's mission and vision, businesses can attract top talent who are committed to working for organizations that prioritize fairness and equal opportunities for all.

- **Brand Reputation**: A company that demonstrates a genuine commitment to DEI through its mission and vision is likely to enhance its brand reputation. Customers and clients increasingly expect the businesses they support to reflect their values, including promoting diversity and inclusion. A clear commitment to these values helps build trust and loyalty, creating stronger relationships with both employees and customers.

- **Alignment with Business Objectives**: When DEI is embedded into the company's mission and vision, it becomes a natural part of the business strategy. Companies can align diversity goals with key performance indicators (KPIs), making DEI an essential driver of organizational performance. This alignment ensures that diversity isn't a siloed effort but rather an integrated component of the company's long-term growth and success.

How to Embed DEI into Mission and Vision

- **Involve Leadership in the Process**: The first step in embedding DEI into the company's mission and vision is to ensure that leadership is fully committed. Leaders should collaborate with diverse teams to understand the importance of DEI and how it will benefit the company's culture and operations. Their commitment should be evident in the language used within the mission and vision statements.

- **Be Specific and Action-Oriented**: Rather than using generic statements about "valuing diversity," be specific about what the company is striving for. This could include creating a more diverse talent pool, fostering an inclusive culture, providing equal opportunities for career advancement, or promoting diversity in leadership. Specificity ensures that the goals are actionable and measurable.

- **Align DEI with Organizational Priorities**: Ensure that DEI goals support and align with the company's overall business strategy. This means identifying how diversity and inclusion contribute to key business objectives such as innovation, market growth, customer satisfaction, and financial performance. Integrating DEI into the business strategy should be seen as a mutually reinforcing effort.

- **Regularly Review and Update**: DEI goals and strategies should not remain static. As the company grows and the external environment changes, regularly reviewing and updating the mission and vision is essential. This ensures that the organization continues to adapt and respond to evolving societal norms, employee needs, and business opportunities.

- **Communicate and Live the Values**: Once DEI goals are integrated into the mission and vision, it's essential to communicate these values to all stakeholders, from employees to customers and partners. Leaders should model inclusive behaviors and demonstrate a commitment to these values in everyday actions. This creates a culture where DEI is not just a statement on paper but a living, breathing part of the organization.

In conclusion, embedding DEI into the mission and vision is a crucial step toward creating a workplace where diversity is celebrated, equity is prioritized, and inclusion is the norm. It's not enough to simply state the intention—organizations must live out these values in every aspect of their operations. By making DEI an integral part of the company's strategy, businesses can unlock new opportunities for growth, innovation, and success while also fostering an environment where all employees can thrive.

2. Make DEI a Leadership Priority

When diversity, equity, and inclusion (DEI) are appropriately aligned with business goals, leadership must take an active and intentional role in prioritizing these initiatives. It's not enough for DEI to be a stated value; it must be woven into the very fabric of the company's operations, goals, and strategic vision. This alignment requires leadership at every level to step up and champion DEI efforts, ensuring that diversity is a consistent and visible priority across all areas of the business.

Active Leadership Involvement

For DEI to succeed, leaders must model the behavior they expect from their teams. It's essential for leaders to not only talk about the importance of diversity but to demonstrate their commitment through actions. This includes discussing DEI initiatives in executive meetings, prioritizing these efforts in business planning, and ensuring that diversity and inclusion are integral to the company's culture. When leaders consistently speak to the value of diversity in shaping the organization's success, it creates a ripple effect that encourages others within the organization to do the same.

Incorporating DEI into Performance Reviews

Just as financial and operational goals are tracked and evaluated, DEI objectives must be integrated into performance reviews for leaders at all levels. By setting clear DEI targets and incorporating them into annual evaluations, companies hold leaders accountable for progress toward these goals. This could mean measuring the diversity of their teams, evaluating how inclusive their leadership style is, or assessing how they have contributed to fostering an environment of equity and belonging. When leaders are held accountable for DEI, it becomes clear that these goals are just as important as any other business metric.

Embedding DEI into Strategic Planning

Incorporating DEI into business planning is a crucial step in making it an organizational priority. As leaders strategize for the future of the company, they must actively ensure that DEI is considered in the decision-making process. This means asking critical questions: How will new initiatives impact diverse groups? Are there opportunities to improve representation at leadership levels? How can we ensure that all employees feel supported and have equal access to growth opportunities? By embedding DEI into strategic discussions, leaders ensure that diversity is not an afterthought but a driving force behind the company's growth and success.

Holding Leaders Accountable for DEI Outcomes

Leaders should be held just as accountable for DEI goals as they are for financial performance or operational efficiency. This means tracking and evaluating their contributions to diversity, equity, and inclusion over time. Accountability can take many forms, from setting and achieving diversity targets to creating an inclusive team culture or implementing programs that support underrepresented groups. Holding leaders accountable for DEI outcomes reinforces the idea that inclusivity is not just a "nice-to-have" but an essential element of the company's success. As the organization's top leaders are expected to deliver on DEI goals, it sets a powerful example for others in the company to follow suit.

Creating a Culture of Responsibility

Leaders also play a pivotal role in creating a culture of responsibility around DEI. By embedding these principles into the daily operations of the company, leaders set the tone for how DEI should be approached at all levels of the organization. This includes fostering open dialogue about bias, creating opportunities for employees to contribute to DEI efforts, and ensuring that the company's policies and practices align with its diversity goals. Leaders must not only communicate the importance of DEI but also create systems for employees to share feedback, voice concerns, and suggest ways to improve inclusivity.

Aligning DEI with business goals requires leadership at every level to prioritize and champion these efforts. It's not enough to passively support diversity initiatives; leaders must be actively involved, embedding DEI into the company's strategic planning, performance reviews, and organizational culture. By holding leaders accountable for DEI outcomes and fostering a culture of inclusivity, organizations can create an environment where diversity is not only valued but is a central driver of business success. Ultimately, when leadership prioritizes DEI, it sets a clear expectation that diversity, equity, and inclusion are critical to the company's long-term growth and prosperity.

3. **Measure and Track Progress**

Setting clear, measurable goals for diversity is essential in creating a strong connection between DEI initiatives and the broader objectives of the company. Without clear goals, DEI efforts can feel fragmented or disconnected from the organization's overall strategy. When diversity goals are explicitly defined, they serve as both a roadmap and a measure of success, ensuring that the initiatives are not just aspirational but also actionable and aligned with the business's priorities. Whether the focus is on improving representation in leadership roles, diversifying the talent pipeline, enhancing employee experiences related to inclusion and belonging, or addressing specific disparities, having a clear framework for measurement helps demonstrate progress and accountability.

To make these goals impactful and relevant, it's essential to break them down into specific, actionable outcomes. For instance, a goal might be to increase the representation of women or people of color in senior leadership roles by a certain percentage over a defined period. Similarly, the company might set targets around the recruitment of underrepresented talent in particular job categories or departments, or it might focus on improving retention rates among marginalized groups through tailored support and development programs. By setting such goals, the company can establish a clear direction for its DEI efforts and define success in concrete terms.

Tracking progress is absolutely critical to ensuring that DEI efforts are making an impact. To do this effectively, companies should leverage both qualitative and quantitative data. Quantitative data, such as demographic breakdowns of the workforce, hiring patterns, and promotion rates, allows organizations to objectively track how diverse their teams are at various levels and how diversity is evolving over time. Meanwhile, qualitative data gathered through employee surveys, focus groups, and feedback sessions helps to measure the effectiveness of inclusion efforts and the sense of belonging among different employee groups. This combination of data allows the company to evaluate not only the "what" of its diversity metrics but also the "why" behind the numbers—helping to paint a more holistic picture of organizational health and progress.

However, collecting data is only part of the equation. The findings need to be communicated transparently throughout the organization. Transparency fosters trust and accountability and ensures that all stakeholders—employees, managers, and leadership—understand where the company stands in relation to its DEI goals. By openly sharing progress, challenges, and the steps being taken to address gaps, leadership can engage employees in the ongoing process of change. Regular updates in company-wide meetings, internal newsletters, or even dedicated DEI reports can ensure that the entire organization is aligned and working toward the same objectives.

Additionally, sharing both successes and areas for improvement creates an environment of learning and growth. It encourages a culture where feedback is embraced, and all employees understand that DEI is a shared responsibility. This open dialogue also helps identify potential barriers or biases that may not be immediately apparent and empowers individuals at all levels of the organization to contribute to solutions.

In conclusion, setting clear, measurable goals for diversity and tracking progress with both qualitative and quantitative metrics is fundamental to integrating DEI into the broader business strategy. By committing to transparency and regularly sharing insights, organizations can maintain momentum, celebrate achievements, and tackle ongoing challenges. This data-driven approach ensures that DEI is not just a peripheral initiative but a core element of the company's long-term growth, inclusivity, and overall success.

4. Embed DEI into Key Business Processes

Incorporating diversity, equity, and inclusion (DEI) goals into core business functions is essential to building a truly inclusive and equitable workplace. DEI should not be a peripheral initiative or a one-time project; it must become deeply embedded within the organization's day-to-day operations and long-term strategy. By weaving DEI into critical business functions such as recruitment, employee development, and decision-making processes, organizations can create a culture where diversity isn't just acknowledged but actively cultivated and celebrated.

Recruitment: Building a Diverse Talent Pipeline

One of the most powerful ways to promote DEI is through the recruitment process. Hiring teams must be equipped with the tools, knowledge, and awareness to actively seek and attract a diverse talent pool. This includes:

- **Inclusive Hiring Practices**: Ensure that job descriptions are written in an inclusive and non-discriminatory manner. Avoid language that may inadvertently discourage particular groups from applying. For example, using gender-neutral terms and highlighting the company's commitment to diversity in the job listing can make a big difference.

- **Bias-Free Interviewing**: Train hiring managers to recognize their own biases and adopt structured, standardized interview processes. This reduces the influence of unconscious bias and ensures that all candidates are assessed based on their skills and qualifications, not personal characteristics or stereotypes.

- **Diverse Candidate Pools**: Actively source candidates from a variety of backgrounds, experiences, and demographics. Use multiple channels to find talent, such as community organizations, job boards that cater to underrepresented groups, and professional associations focused on diversity. Partner with universities and colleges that have strong diversity programs and ensure that the hiring process is accessible to people with disabilities or those who face other barriers.

- **Inclusive Selection Panels**: Assemble diverse interview panels to ensure that hiring decisions are made through a range of perspectives. This not only minimizes bias but also sends a message to candidates that the organization values diverse voices at all levels of the business.

By aligning recruitment strategies with DEI goals, organizations can build a more inclusive workforce from the ground up, fostering an environment where diverse perspectives contribute to innovation, creativity, and overall business success.

Employee Development: Investing in Growth for All

Once diverse talent has been recruited, organizations must ensure that employees have the resources, support, and opportunities they need to succeed and advance. Employee development should be a critical part of the DEI framework, offering mentorship, training, and pathways to leadership for all employees, particularly those from underrepresented groups.

- **Mentorship Programs**: Implement mentorship initiatives that pair employees from diverse backgrounds with senior leaders or more experienced colleagues. These programs provide valuable guidance, encouragement, and networking opportunities that can help individuals navigate their careers, develop new skills, and gain visibility within the organization. Special attention should be given to ensuring that mentors and mentees come from diverse groups, allowing for a broad exchange of perspectives and experiences.

- **Leadership Development Programs**: To build a diverse leadership pipeline, organizations should create opportunities for underrepresented employees to develop leadership skills. This might include providing leadership training, sponsorship, and opportunities for high-visibility projects. By ensuring that employees from all backgrounds have access to these opportunities, organizations can begin to dismantle the systemic barriers that often prevent marginalized groups from advancing to leadership positions.

- **Bias in Performance Reviews**: Establish clear criteria for performance evaluations and ensure that all employees are assessed based on their merits, contributions, and goals. Use 360-degree feedback mechanisms, where employees can provide input on the performance of their peers and managers. This holistic approach to performance reviews helps minimize individual bias and promotes a more balanced, equitable evaluation process.

- **Career Pathing and Advancement**: Regularly review career development plans to ensure that employees are aware of the opportunities available for growth within the organization. Make sure that employees from underrepresented groups are included in these conversations and have a clear roadmap for career advancement.

By investing in the development of all employees and ensuring equitable access to growth opportunities, organizations can help underrepresented groups rise to leadership positions and ensure that the workforce reflects a wide range of talents, experiences, and perspectives.

Decision-Making: Creating an Inclusive Framework for Growth

DEI should also play a pivotal role in the decision making processes at all levels of the organization. Whether it's about setting company-wide policies, shaping team strategies, or determining new product launches, decisions should be made through an inclusive lens that accounts for the diverse perspectives of all stakeholders.

- **Inclusive Leadership Teams**: Encourage diverse leadership teams that bring varied experiences, skills, and viewpoints to the table. Diverse teams make more informed, innovative decisions because they consider a wider range of options and anticipate challenges from multiple angles. It's essential to ensure that decision-making bodies reflect the diversity of the employee base, the customers, and the communities in which the business operates.

- **Inclusive Policy Making**: When developing new policies, companies should consult with employees from different backgrounds, departments, and experiences. This ensures that policies don't inadvertently exclude or disadvantage certain groups. For example, when implementing remote work policies, companies should consider the needs of parents, caregivers, and those with disabilities to ensure that these policies are equitable and inclusive.

- **Employee Resource Groups (ERGs)**: ERGs can be a valuable resource in decision-making, offering insights and feedback from various demographic groups. They serve as a sounding board for policies, initiatives, and projects, ensuring that they are inclusive and aligned with the diverse needs of the workforce. Involving ERGs in the decision-making process fosters a sense of ownership and belonging among employees and allows the organization to make more informed, empathetic decisions.

- **Inclusive Business Strategy**: Ensure that the company's strategic direction incorporates DEI considerations into every decision. This can involve anything from targeting new customer segments to developing products and services that cater to a more diverse audience. Businesses that adopt an inclusive strategy are more likely to understand and meet the needs of a broad customer base, ultimately increasing their market reach and customer satisfaction.

DEI is the DNA of the Company

When DEI is integrated into the company's core functions, it becomes part of the organization's DNA—something that is fundamental to how the business operates at every level. It shapes the culture, drives behavior, and informs decisions. When diversity is built into recruitment, employee development, and decision-making processes, it sends a clear message that the company values inclusion not as a checkbox to tick but as an integral aspect of how the business functions.

By committing to DEI in these fundamental areas, organizations create a workplace where people feel seen, heard, and valued. This not only improves employee morale and retention but also contributes to more significant innovation, better decision-making, and long-term success. The result is a more resilient, forward-thinking company that is prepared to adapt to an ever-changing world. DEI should no longer be an afterthought or a trend; it should be a pillar of your business strategy, helping to guide your company toward a more inclusive, equitable, and prosperous future.

5. **Focus on the Bottom Line**

Many companies still perceive Diversity, Equity, and Inclusion (DEI) as merely a 'nice-to-have' initiative, something that is often added as an afterthought or driven by external pressures. However, when DEI is aligned with the bottom line and integrated into a company's core business strategy, it transforms from a superficial effort into a powerful driver of organizational success. Far from being just a trend or a passing fad, DEI has become a critical factor in ensuring companies remain competitive and innovative in today's global, fast-changing marketplace.

The Power of Diverse Teams

Diverse teams bring a rich variety of perspectives, experiences, and skill sets to the table, and this diversity can be the catalyst for innovation. When people from different backgrounds, cultures, genders, and perspectives come together, they are more likely to approach problems from various angles, generate fresh ideas, and offer creative solutions that would not emerge in a homogeneous group. This results in a more dynamic and adaptable workforce, one that is better equipped to navigate complex challenges and seize opportunities in an increasingly competitive environment.

Moreover, diverse teams often make better decisions. According to research from McKinsey & Company, companies with more diverse executive teams are 33% more likely to outperform their peers on profitability and above-average returns. This is because diverse teams have a broader range of insights to draw from, which leads to more well-rounded, comprehensive decision-making. They are less likely to fall into groupthink, where a lack of diversity leads to narrow viewpoints and missed opportunities.

The Business Case for DEI

Numerous studies have demonstrated that diverse companies are more likely to outperform their competitors financially. For instance, a 2020 McKinsey report found that companies in the top quartile for gender and ethnic diversity on executive teams were 25% more likely to have above-average profitability than those in the bottom quartile. Another study by Credit Suisse revealed that companies with at least one female board member had better returns on equity, highlighting how diversity in leadership positively impacts financial performance.

This is not a coincidence. Companies that embrace diversity create work environments that attract top talent from a wide range of backgrounds. This increases the quality of the talent pool and fosters a culture of high performance. Moreover, a commitment to DEI can enhance customer satisfaction by ensuring that the workforce reflects the diversity of the customer base. When customers see that a company values diversity, they are more likely to feel connected to the brand, which can lead to higher customer loyalty and improved sales.

DEI as a Long-Term Growth Strategy

When leadership aligns DEI efforts with broader business outcomes—such as customer satisfaction, market share, and profitability—it becomes an essential part of the company's long-term growth strategy. DEI isn't just about filling quotas or checking boxes; it's about creating a business model that leverages diverse perspectives and experiences to drive innovation, improve performance, and enhance customer relationships. It's about creating a company culture that attracts and retains top talent, fosters creativity, and positions the organization as a forward-thinking leader in its industry.

For instance, aligning DEI with customer satisfaction can lead to the development of products and services that cater to a broader audience, addressing the needs and preferences of diverse demographic groups. This can give companies a competitive edge in expanding their market share and increasing revenue. Similarly, fostering a culture of inclusion within the workplace boosts employee morale and engagement, which in turn reduces turnover rates and lowers recruitment costs.

Furthermore, diverse teams tend to be more adaptable and resilient, qualities that are crucial for navigating an unpredictable business environment. In today's fast-paced world, companies that can embrace change, adapt to new trends, and quickly pivot when necessary are more likely to thrive. By integrating DEI into their core business strategies, companies are better equipped to manage disruption and seize new opportunities.

The Bottom Line: A Crucial Investment

In conclusion, DEI should no longer be viewed as a peripheral initiative but as a critical component of a company's overall business strategy. When DEI is aligned with business outcomes like profitability, customer satisfaction, and market share, it becomes a driving force for organizational success. By cultivating diverse teams and fostering an inclusive culture, companies can unlock innovation, improve decision-making, and gain a competitive advantage in their industry. In today's interconnected, globalized world, organizations that prioritize diversity and inclusion are more likely to experience long-term growth and sustainable success. As a result, DEI should be seen not as a cost or a "nice-to-have," but as a wise, strategic investment in the future of the company.

Creating a Sustainable DEI Framework

To ensure that diversity, equity, and inclusion are not just short-lived initiatives, they must be supported by a sustainable framework that is adaptable, measurable, and embedded into the culture of the organization. Creating such a framework requires both structural and cultural changes that are maintained over time. Here's how to build a DEI framework that stands the test of time:

- **Develop Clear Policies and Guidelines**: A sustainable DEI framework begins with clear, written policies that reflect the organization's commitment to diversity and inclusion. These policies should outline the company's stance on equity, fairness, and anti-discrimination, providing guidelines for how these principles will be implemented. For example, policies can set expectations for behavior, procedures for reporting discrimination, and steps for conflict resolution.

- **Provide Ongoing Education and Training**: A commitment to DEI requires continuous learning. Implement regular training programs that cover unconscious bias, inclusive leadership, cultural competence, and other DEI-related topics. These programs should be designed to engage employees at all levels and should evolve as new insights and best practices emerge. For instance, initial training might focus on raising awareness of bias, but over time, it should include more advanced topics like dismantling systemic inequalities or fostering a truly inclusive workplace culture.

- **Create Accountability Systems**: Holding people accountable for their actions is crucial for a sustainable DEI framework. This means embedding accountability into performance reviews, leadership development, and everyday business operations. Leaders should be evaluated not only on financial or operational performance but also on their ability to drive DEI initiatives. Employees should feel that they are supported in their efforts to contribute to a diverse and inclusive culture, and there should be consequences for failing to meet DEI goals.

- **Foster Employee Engagement and Ownership**: For DEI efforts to be sustainable, employees must feel personally connected to the mission. Encourage employee involvement through DEI committees, resource groups, or volunteer opportunities. Employees can serve as DEI ambassadors or participate in workshops and initiatives that promote inclusivity. This fosters a sense of ownership and ensures that DEI becomes everyone's responsibility, not just that of the leadership team.

- **Embed DEI into the Company's Culture**: A sustainable DEI framework cannot exist without a culture that values and practices inclusivity. To create such a culture, leadership must consistently model inclusive behaviors, celebrate diversity, and recognize contributions from all employees. DEI should be part of how the company operates on a day-to-day basis, from team collaboration to customer interactions. Creating a culture where people feel they belong, are valued, and can thrive is essential to embedding DEI into the organization's long-term strategy.

- **Regularly Assess and Evolve the Framework**: Just as the business environment changes, so too must the DEI framework evolve. Regularly assess the framework's effectiveness through employee surveys, focus groups, and external audits. Use the data to refine and adjust strategies, policies, and goals. An adaptable framework ensures that DEI efforts remain relevant and impactful as the organization grows and as societal norms continue to shift.

Why This Matters: A Long-Term Vision for Diversity and Inclusion

Embedding bias reduction into organizational strategy and creating a sustainable Diversity, Equity, and

Inclusion (DEI) framework goes far beyond being a passing trend or a box to check. It represents a critical shift toward establishing a genuinely inclusive workplace culture, where all employees—regardless of their background, identity, or experiences—are empowered to thrive. In a world where organizational success is increasingly intertwined with diversity, aligning DEI with the strategic goals and core values of the company isn't just an ideal; it's an essential step toward building a resilient, future-proof organization.

When DEI is woven into an organization's fabric, it doesn't just exist on paper; it influences daily operations, decision-making, and the overall workplace environment. From recruitment to leadership practices to team dynamics and customer relations, every touchpoint is impacted by a DEI strategy that is both intentional and embedded within the company's mission. This ensures that diversity isn't merely a buzzword but a lived experience for employees, driving them to engage meaningfully with their work and contribute to the company's success.

Organizations that go the extra mile in committing to long-term DEI goals foster a sense of belonging and fairness, which translates to tangible business advantages. Employees who feel valued and included are more likely to be engaged, motivated, and loyal. This leads to improved retention rates and a reduction in turnover, which can be costly and disruptive. Moreover, diverse teams bring a variety of perspectives and ideas, driving innovation and enhancing the company's ability to adapt in a fast-changing marketplace. The collective result is a more agile organization, better equipped to solve complex challenges and seize new opportunities.

It's critical to understand that DEI is no longer a "nice-to-have" or an optional initiative—it is an investment in the organization's future. Fostering a diverse and inclusive environment will not only enhance the organization's reputation. Still, it will also provide a competitive edge in attracting top talent, appealing to a diverse customer base, and navigating the global economy. By investing in DEI, companies position themselves as leaders in social responsibility, showing their commitment to fairness, equality, and justice in all areas of business.

As you integrate DEI into your organizational strategy, recognize that this commitment is not just a business tactic; it is a moral imperative. In today's increasingly interconnected world, organizations are under greater scrutiny, and their commitment to social issues is more critical than ever. A focus on DEI can serve as a catalyst for broader societal change while also setting the stage for business growth and transformation.

By making DEI a central part of your organizational strategy, you are not simply fulfilling a corporate responsibility but shaping an environment where every employee feels empowered to contribute their best. This investment in people and culture isn't a one-time project—it's an ongoing journey that, when done right, will ensure the long-term success and resilience of your organization. Through this commitment to diversity, equity, and inclusion, your company will build the foundation for a more sustainable, inclusive future— one where growth is driven by a team that feels valued, heard and included.

ENGAGING EMPLOYEES IN THE DEI JOURNEY

Establishing a diverse and inclusive workplace is a process rather than a final goal. All employees, from entry-level workers to top executives, must actively participate in the process as firms work to address unconscious prejudice and advance diversity, equality, and inclusion (DEI). This involvement aims to promote a shared commitment to inclusion, empowerment, and transformation rather than merely enacting laws or obeying directives.

Building Buy-In Across All Levels of the Organization

Making sure that buy-in is developed throughout the entire firm is one of the most challenging tasks in attaining long-term DEI success. Results are more significant and long-lasting when workers at all levels—from CEOs to front-line staff—understand the value of DEI and feel invested in its outcomes.

1. Leadership Commitment

Engagement starts at the top, and the role of leadership in fostering diversity, equity, and inclusion (DEI) cannot be overstated. Leaders are the architects of organizational culture, and their actions set the tone for what is valued and prioritized. For DEI initiatives to thrive, leadership must go beyond passive endorsement and actively champion these efforts through both words and actions.

Demonstrating Commitment Through Action

Leadership commitment to DEI must be visible and intentional. It begins with allocating the necessary resources—financial, human, and time—to support DEI initiatives. This could involve funding for training programs, creating positions such as a Chief Diversity Officer, or investing in tools to track progress and measure impact. By ensuring DEI efforts are adequately resourced, leaders signal their seriousness about achieving meaningful change.

Leading by Example

Leaders must embody the values of inclusivity and equity in their everyday behaviors. This includes being transparent about their own biases, admitting mistakes, and taking responsibility for their actions. When leaders openly acknowledge areas for personal growth and improvement, they create a culture of psychological safety that encourages others to do the same. For example, a leader who admits to unintentionally overlooking diverse perspectives in a decision-making process and takes corrective action demonstrates humility and a commitment to inclusivity.

Accountability is Non-Negotiable

Leadership accountability is crucial in maintaining momentum for DEI initiatives. This means setting clear goals, publicly committing to them, and regularly reviewing progress. Leaders should hold themselves to the same standards they expect of others, ensuring that DEI is not seen as an optional add-on but as a core organizational value. Whether it's publishing diversity metrics, participating in training sessions alongside employees, or taking an active role in mentoring underrepresented team members, accountability from the top establishes credibility and trust.

Making DEI a Leadership Priority

DEI must be integrated into the broader leadership agenda, not siloed as a separate initiative. When inclusivity becomes part of strategic planning, decision-making, and performance evaluations, it demonstrates that DEI is central to the organization's mission and long-term success. Leaders should advocate for diverse representation in leadership roles, establish mentorship programs, and actively seek out underrepresented voices when forming teams or committees.

Communicating the Vision

Leadership must develop a clear, compelling vision for DEI. This involves articulating why DEI matters to the organization, how it aligns with its values, and the specific steps being taken to drive progress. Regular updates on DEI initiatives, challenges, and successes keep the workforce informed and engaged. Leaders should foster open dialogues by inviting feedback, addressing concerns, and celebrating wins. When communication is consistent and authentic, it reinforces the organization's commitment to inclusivity.

Inspiring the Organization

When leaders actively champion DEI, they inspire others to join the journey. A passionate leader who advocates for equitable policies participates in community initiatives or supports employee resource groups (ERGs) can galvanize the workforce. This ripple effect creates a culture where inclusivity becomes everyone's responsibility.

Addressing Resistance

Leaders must also be prepared to address resistance to DEI efforts. Change can be uncomfortable, and some employees may feel threatened by new initiatives. Strong leadership involves listening to concerns, addressing misconceptions, and reinforcing the importance of DEI for the organization's growth and success. Leaders should provide clarity about how inclusivity benefits not only marginalized groups but the entire workforce, fostering a sense of shared purpose.

The Impact of Leadership Engagement

When leaders are fully engaged in DEI, the results are transformative. Their visible commitment sends a clear message that inclusivity is not just a checkbox exercise but a core value. Employees are more likely to embrace DEI efforts when they see leadership taking the lead, creating a culture where everyone feels seen, valued, and respected.

Leadership engagement is the foundation of a successful DEI journey. By prioritizing action, accountability, and communication, leaders create a ripple effect that inspires the entire organization to move toward a more inclusive, equitable future.

2. Communication is Key

Clear, transparent, and frequent communication is the cornerstone of building genuine buy-in for Diversity, Equity, and Inclusion (DEI) initiatives. To foster trust and commitment, organizations must go beyond generic statements and articulate the deeper "why" behind their DEI efforts. This involves connecting DEI objectives to the organization's mission, values, and long-term goals. Employees should understand not only that DEI matters but also how it drives innovation, strengthens collaboration, and fosters a more positive workplace culture.

Explaining the Importance of DEI

Organizations need to clearly outline why DEI is critical—not just as a moral or ethical imperative but also as a strategic advantage. This means highlighting how inclusivity enhances team performance, drives creativity, and attracts a broader talent pool. By framing DEI as integral to the company's success, employees are more likely to view it as a shared responsibility rather than an external mandate.

For example, sharing stories or case studies that illustrate the tangible impact of DEI—such as how inclusive practices have improved customer satisfaction, led to groundbreaking ideas, or resolved workplace challenges—can bring abstract concepts to life. These real-world examples make the message relatable and underscore the benefits for individuals, teams, and the organization as a whole.

Aligning DEI with Company Values

To build lasting commitment, DEI efforts must be deeply embedded in the organization's values and vision. Employees are more likely to engage when they see that DEI aligns with the principles the company already claims to uphold. For instance, if a company values innovation, leaders can explain how diverse perspectives fuel creative problem-solving. If teamwork is a core value, they can highlight how inclusivity fosters collaboration and mutual respect.

This alignment must be more than rhetorical. Leaders should demonstrate through actions—such as policy changes, resource allocation, and public commitments—that DEI is a non-negotiable priority. When employees witness DEI being championed in decision-making and daily practices, they are more likely to feel inspired to contribute.

Establishing Clear Goals and Actions

Employees need to see that DEI initiatives are not vague aspirations but well-defined plans with actionable steps. Organizations should outline specific goals such as increasing representation in leadership roles, closing pay gaps, or ensuring equitable access to development opportunities. These goals should be accompanied by concrete actions and timelines, demonstrating that the organization is serious about driving measurable change.

Transparency about these goals also builds accountability. Regular updates on progress, whether through team meetings, newsletters, or dedicated DEI dashboards, help keep employees informed. Importantly, organizations should be candid about challenges, acknowledging where progress is slower than expected and outlining steps to overcome obstacles. This honesty builds trust and reinforces the message that DEI is an evolving journey, not a box to check.

Encouraging Feedback and Open Dialogue

Authentic engagement thrives in an environment where employees feel heard and valued. Organizations should actively invite questions, concerns, and suggestions about DEI initiatives, creating spaces where employees can express themselves without fear of judgment or reprisal. This could include:

- **Listening sessions:** Small group discussions to explore employee perspectives on inclusion and bias.

- **Anonymous surveys:** Tools for gathering honest feedback on DEI progress and areas needing improvement.

- **DEI committees or task forces:** Groups that include diverse representation to ensure different voices shape the organization's efforts.

Leaders must also model openness by responding constructively to feedback. When employees see their input leading to tangible changes, they feel more invested in the process. Open dialogue fosters mutual respect and allows the organization to address blind spots or unintended consequences in its DEI initiatives.

Fostering Two-Way Communication

Communication is most effective when it's a two-way street. Leaders and managers should not only share updates but also actively seek out and listen to employee experiences. Stories of exclusion, success, or personal growth can offer invaluable insights and inspire others to reflect on their role in creating an inclusive culture.

This type of engagement also humanizes DEI efforts. Employees are more likely to feel a personal connection to the cause when they see colleagues and leaders sharing authentic stories about their own DEI journeys—whether that involves learning from past biases, championing equity, or advocating for change.

The Power of Consistency

Consistency in communication reinforces the message that DEI is not a passing trend but a core organizational commitment. Regular touchpoints, such as quarterly DEI updates or monthly team discussions, help maintain momentum and ensure that inclusion remains top-of-mind. Communication should also adapt as the organization evolves, addressing new challenges and celebrating fresh milestones.

In essence, clear, transparent, and frequent communication is more than a strategy—it is a vital component of creating a culture of trust and accountability. By explaining the importance of DEI, aligning it with company values, establishing clear goals, and fostering open dialogue, organizations can inspire employees to become active participants in the journey. When employees are informed, engaged, and empowered, they become champions for change, driving a collective effort to create a truly inclusive workplace.

3. Inclusivity in Decision-Making

Engaging employees in the decision-making process around diversity, equity, and inclusion (DEI) initiatives is one of the most effective ways to foster a sense of ownership and commitment. When employees actively contribute to shaping the policies, programs, and training that impact them, they feel valued, respected, and heard. This involvement transforms

DEI from a top-down directive into a shared mission that unites the organization.

Fostering Meaningful Engagement

To achieve authentic engagement, employees must have a platform to voice their ideas, concerns, and experiences. This can be accomplished through a variety of mechanisms:

- **Focus Groups:** Small, diverse groups of employees can be brought together to discuss specific DEI-related topics. These sessions allow for candid conversations about workplace challenges, cultural dynamics, and potential solutions. Focus groups provide valuable insights into the unique needs and perspectives of employees across different demographics and roles.

- **Surveys and Feedback Mechanisms:** Anonymous surveys are a powerful tool for collecting honest input from a broad range of employees. By asking targeted questions about their experiences and perceptions of DEI within the workplace, organizations can identify areas for improvement. Open feedback channels, such as suggestion boxes or online platforms, also enable employees to share ideas and concerns in real time.

- **DEI Task Forces:** Creating task forces composed of representatives from various departments, levels, and backgrounds ensures that different voices are heard. These groups can collaborate on the design, implementation, and evaluation of DEI initiatives. Task forces empower employees to take an active role in driving change and act as ambassadors for inclusivity within their teams.

- **Workshops and Co-Creation Sessions:** Interactive workshops where employees work together to brainstorm and design DEI strategies can be efficient. These sessions encourage cross-departmental collaboration and allow employees to contribute creatively to the organization's DEI goals.

Creating a Sense of Ownership

When employees see that their input directly influences DEI initiatives, they are more likely to feel a sense of ownership and pride in the outcomes. This sense of ownership has several benefits:

- **Higher Engagement:** Employees who feel included in decision-making are more likely to be emotionally and intellectually invested in the success of the organization's DEI efforts.

- **Increased Accountability:** When employees contribute to shaping policies, they are more likely to hold themselves and others accountable for upholding those standards.

- **Tailored Solutions:** Employee involvement ensures that DEI initiatives are aligned with the real needs and challenges of the workforce, making them more relevant and effective.

Building Trust and Transparency

Involving employees in DEI decision-making is not just about gathering input—it's about building trust and transparency. To maintain this trust, organizations must:

- **Act on Feedback:** Employees need to see that their suggestions are taken seriously. If specific ideas cannot be implemented, explain why and offer alternative solutions to show their input was valued.

- **Provide Updates:** Regularly communicate the progress of DEI initiatives, including milestones achieved and challenges faced. Transparency reinforces the message that employees are integral to the organization's journey.

- **Celebrate Contributions:** Recognize and celebrate employees who actively participate in DEI efforts, whether through formal acknowledgment or informal appreciation. This reinforces the importance of their involvement.

A Collaborative Culture of Inclusion

When employees are involved in shaping DEI policies and practices, the organization fosters a culture of collaboration and shared responsibility. This culture helps to break down silos, build stronger connections among employees, and reinforce the idea that DEI is not just an organizational priority but a collective one.

Ultimately, engaging employees in decision-making creates a workplace where everyone feels empowered to contribute to a more inclusive, equitable, and thriving environment.

4. Providing Education and Awareness

To truly build buy-in for DEI efforts, employees must deeply understand the "why" behind these initiatives. It's not enough to issue mandates or roll out surface-level policies—employees need to grasp the importance of diversity, equity, and inclusion on both a personal and organizational level. This begins with an education that sheds light on critical issues such as unconscious bias, systemic inequalities, and the tangible benefits of a diverse and inclusive workplace.

Connecting DEI to Real-World Impact

Employees are more likely to engage when they see the real-world implications of DEI. Education should highlight how biases manifest in everyday interactions, hiring decisions, and workplace dynamics. Using concrete examples—such as case studies, testimonials, or even anonymized internal data—can help employees understand how these issues affect them, their colleagues, and the organization as a whole. By making

DEI relatable and relevant, employees can better see its value beyond abstract principles.

Continuous and Interactive Training

DEI education is not a one-time event; it must be an ongoing process embedded in the organizational culture. Interactive workshops, role-playing scenarios, and open discussions create safe spaces for employees to explore their own biases, ask difficult questions, and learn collaboratively. Regular training sessions can focus on different aspects of DEI, ensuring that the learning process evolves and adapts over time. Incorporating real-life examples and industry-specific challenges can make the training more engaging and impactful.

Pro Tip: Incorporate micro-learning modules—short, focused training sessions employees can access on demand. This flexibility allows for sustained engagement without overwhelming employees' schedules.

Empowering Employees to Take Ownership

When employees are equipped with knowledge, they feel empowered to become active participants in the DEI journey. This involves creating an environment where they are encouraged to reflect on their own experiences and biases, engage in meaningful dialogue, and take actionable steps toward inclusivity. For example, employees can be invited to contribute to DEI task forces, lead initiatives within their teams, or participate in mentorship programs that foster cross-cultural understanding.

Making Learning a Two-Way Street

Organizations often approach DEI education as a top-down initiative, but to truly embed it into the culture, it should be a shared responsibility. Leaders and employees alike should view the learning process as collaborative. Leaders can share their journeys, challenges, and growth, demonstrating vulnerability and commitment to the cause. Employees, in turn, can contribute their perspectives, providing valuable insights into how DEI efforts resonate at all levels of the organization.

Highlighting the Business Case and Beyond

Education should also address the practical benefits of DEI for the organization. Studies consistently show that diverse teams perform better, foster more significant innovation, and improve decision-making. However, it's equally important to emphasize the human case for DEI: creating a workplace where everyone feels valued, respected, and empowered to contribute their best. By balancing the business case with the ethical imperative, employees are more likely to align with DEI as a core organizational value.

Measuring and Celebrating Progress

Organizations should measure and share progress to reinforce the importance of DEI. Regular updates on DEI milestones, improvements in diversity metrics, and success stories can motivate employees to stay engaged. Recognizing and celebrating individual and team contributions to DEI efforts creates a sense of collective achievement and reinforces the idea that DEI is a shared responsibility.

By fostering a culture where employees are empowered to learn, grow, and evolve, organizations can transform DEI from a top-down directive into a dynamic, shared journey. Continuous, interactive education tied to real-world impact helps employees internalize the importance of DEI and commit to it wholeheartedly. When employees understand the "why" behind DEI and see themselves as active participants in the process, the organization can create a thriving, inclusive workplace where diversity is not just an ideal but a lived reality.

5. Aligning DEI with Organizational Goals

DEI (Diversity, Equity, and Inclusion) must transcend buzzwords and surface-level initiatives to become an integral part of an organization's foundation. It should be deeply embedded in the organization's core values, mission, and long-term strategic goals. When DEI is fully integrated, it signals that inclusivity is not just a "nice-to-have" but a critical component of the organization's identity, purpose, and pathway to sustainable success.

Aligning DEI with Core Values and Mission

Organizations with a clear commitment to DEI tie their initiatives to their fundamental principles and mission statements. This alignment ensures that DEI is reflected in every aspect of the organization, from decision-making and policy creation to customer interactions and community engagement. By rooting DEI in the organization's mission, leaders send a powerful message: inclusion and equity are not optional—they are part of the DNA that drives how the organization operates and grows.

Making DEI a Strategic Imperative

Incorporating DEI into the organization's long-term goals is essential for sustainable impact. This means going beyond standalone projects or temporary campaigns to embed DEI into broader objectives such as talent development, market expansion, and innovation strategies. For example:

- **Talent Acquisition and Retention:** Building diverse teams and fostering an inclusive culture helps attract top talent and reduces turnover.

- **Market Growth:** Embracing diversity equips organizations to better understand and serve global and multicultural markets, fostering stronger connections with customers.

- **Innovation and Creativity:** Teams with diverse perspectives consistently outperform homogenous groups in problem-solving and creativity, driving innovation across industries.

Communicating DEI as a Business Advantage

When DEI is seamlessly integrated, employees can clearly see how it contributes to individual and organizational success. Research has shown that inclusive organizations outperform their peers in key areas, including:

- **Innovation:** Diverse teams bring a broader range of perspectives and ideas, fostering creativity and groundbreaking solutions.

- **Employee Satisfaction:** Inclusive workplaces create environments where employees feel valued, respected, and empowered, leading to higher engagement and morale.

- **Performance and Profitability:** Companies that prioritize DEI often see improved financial performance, as inclusivity drives better decision-making and team dynamics.

Organizations should regularly communicate these benefits through storytelling, case studies, and data-driven insights, helping employees connect the dots between DEI initiatives and tangible outcomes. For instance, sharing examples of how diverse leadership has driven a successful product launch or how inclusive practices have strengthened customer loyalty can help employees feel proud to be part of the DEI journey.

Creating Accountability and Transparency

A fully integrated DEI strategy also involves building mechanisms for accountability. Organizations should set measurable goals, track progress, and report on results to ensure DEI initiatives are not only implemented but sustained. Transparency in these efforts builds trust, demonstrating to employees that the organization is serious about its commitment to inclusion and equity.

Fostering a Sense of Belonging

Ultimately, weaving DEI into the organizational fabric creates an environment where every employee feels a sense of belonging. It's a place where diverse talents and perspectives are celebrated, equitable opportunities are accessible, and inclusion is a shared responsibility. When employees see that DEI is not an afterthought but a driving force behind the organization's vision and actions, they are more likely to embrace and champion these efforts themselves.

By positioning DEI as a non-negotiable element of its identity, an organization sets the stage for meaningful change that benefits employees, stakeholders, and the broader community. It becomes a space where innovation thrives, creativity flourishes, and everyone has the opportunity to contribute to shared success.

Empowering Employees to Become Allies and Advocates

While leadership plays a pivotal role in driving DEI initiatives, empowering employees to become active participants is essential. This involves not only making them aware of their own biases but also giving them the tools and resources to advocate for inclusivity within their teams and across the organization.

- **Encouraging Allyship:** Allyship goes beyond passive support—it requires active engagement and commitment. To empower employees to become allies, organizations must provide the tools and understanding necessary to intervene when they witness bias or inequality. Allyship training can teach employees how to step up in conversations, offer support to marginalized colleagues, and speak out against discriminatory practices. When allies understand their role and how they can contribute to positive change, they help create a safer, more inclusive environment for all.

- **Creating a Supportive Network:** Allies and advocates thrive in a supportive environment where they feel safe to speak out and take action. This can be achieved by fostering a network of employees committed to DEI, where members can share experiences, learn from each other, and offer support. Employee resource groups (ERGs), mentorship programs, and affinity groups can serve as platforms for allies to connect, educate one another, and promote a culture of inclusion across the organization.

- **Recognizing and Rewarding Advocacy:** Recognizing employees who actively contribute to the DEI journey is crucial. Acknowledging the efforts of allies, advocates, and employees who embody inclusive behaviors can inspire others to follow suit. Whether through formal awards, public recognition, or opportunities for career advancement, rewarding advocacy sends a clear message that being an ally is valued by the organization. This encourages employees to continue championing DEI in their day-to-day interactions and to stand up for inclusivity.

- **Providing Platforms for Employee Voice:** Empowerment comes from creating space for employees to share their perspectives, experiences, and ideas. This could be through town halls, feedback sessions, or even informal meetings where employees can raise concerns or suggest improvements. When employees feel their voices are heard and valued, they are more likely to become engaged in promoting DEI and advocating for positive change.

- **Encouraging Bystander Intervention:** A key aspect of empowering employees to advocate for change is encouraging bystander intervention. Employees should be trained to recognize harmful behaviors, such as microaggressions or exclusionary practices, and to know how to intervene appropriately. This includes using positive language, standing up for colleagues, and offering support to those affected. A workplace where bystanders feel empowered to act is one where DEI is reinforced at every level.

The Impact of Engaged Employees on DEI

When employees at all levels of an organization are fully engaged in the diversity, equity, and inclusion (DEI) journey, the results can be nothing short of transformative. They evolve from being mere recipients of company policies to becoming active agents of change. This shift in mindset and behavior drives a ripple effect that touches every facet of the organization—from recruitment and retention to innovation, collaboration, and overall employee morale.

Engagement Fuels Transformation

Engaged employees who truly understand the importance of DEI contribute to a culture that prioritizes respect, equity, and belonging. These individuals don't just follow protocols; they embody the values of inclusivity in their daily interactions. They speak up in support of marginalized colleagues, advocate for fair processes, and challenge biases when they appear. This active participation helps build an environment where everyone feels not only safe but empowered to bring their authentic selves to work.

The benefits of this engagement are multi-dimensional. Employees who feel seen, valued, and respected are more likely to be satisfied with their jobs, fostering loyalty and reducing turnover. Furthermore, inclusivity creates the psychological safety needed for creativity and innovation to thrive. Teams that embrace diverse perspectives and ideas are better equipped to solve complex problems, adapt to change, and outperform their competitors.

The Ripple Effect of Engagement

The impact of employee engagement in the DEI journey extends far beyond individual actions. When inclusivity becomes a shared responsibility, the organization experiences profound cultural and operational shifts. Recruitment processes become more equitable, attracting top talent from a wide range of backgrounds. Performance reviews and promotions are evaluated through an unbiased lens, ensuring that opportunities are distributed fairly. Team dynamics improve as collaboration is built on mutual respect and understanding.

This ripple effect also enhances the organization's reputation externally. Companies that demonstrate a genuine commitment to DEI are seen as forward-thinking and socially responsible, which resonates with customers, clients, and investors alike. By prioritizing DEI, organizations position themselves as leaders in their industry, capable of driving meaningful change both internally and externally.

Empowerment as the Cornerstone of Success

True transformation happens when organizations go beyond surface-level efforts and empower their employees to be allies and advocates for change. This involves providing them with the tools, resources, and opportunities needed to take ownership of DEI initiatives. When employees feel that their voices matter and their actions can drive progress, they are more likely to embrace the journey as their own.

Empowerment also involves creating a culture of accountability, where everyone—from leadership to entry-level staff—shares the responsibility of fostering inclusion. This means encouraging open conversations about bias, celebrating small wins, and remaining transparent about areas for growth. It's about making

DEI a continuous, evolving process rather than a box to check.

Creating Lasting Change

By building buy-in across all levels of the organization and empowering employees to be active participants, companies lay the groundwork for long-term success in their DEI efforts. The key to this success lies in cultivating a culture where inclusion isn't seen as an isolated initiative but as a fundamental value that informs every decision and interaction.

Sustaining this momentum requires intentionality, resilience, and adaptability. Organizations must continuously assess their progress, learn from their setbacks, and remain committed to the journey, even when challenges arise. When inclusivity becomes woven into the fabric of the workplace, it transforms from a goal to a guiding principle—one that drives growth, innovation, and unity.

Ultimately, DEI's true power lies in its ability to create workplaces where everyone feels they belong and can thrive. When every employee feels responsible for fostering inclusion, the organization becomes a stronger, more compassionate, and more innovative force—ready to navigate the complexities of an ever-changing world.

LEADERSHIP DEVELOPMENT FOR INCLUSIVE LEADERSHIP

Strong, competent, and compassionate leadership is the first step in establishing an inclusive workplace. Since they establish the tone for an organization's culture and principles, leaders are the change agents. However, many leaders unwittingly reinforce prejudices because they are unaware of them or lack the necessary resources to deal with them. Organizations must fund training initiatives and encourage actions that advance fairness, trust, and a sense of belonging to cultivate inclusive leadership.

Training Programs for Leaders on Bias Awareness and Inclusion

Leaders cannot tackle what they don't recognize. Bias awareness training serves as a critical starting point to help leaders identify and understand unconscious biases that influence decision-making and workplace interactions. These training programs focus on three key aspects:

1. **Understanding Bias:**

Effective programs begin with an exploration of how unconscious bias operates at the neurological level. Leaders are introduced to the cognitive processes that drive automatic associations and stereotypes, such as the brain's tendency to categorize information quickly for efficiency. These shortcuts, while natural, often lead to biased judgments and assumptions. Through engaging content—such as neuroscience-based explanations, case studies, and practical examples—leaders gain a deeper understanding of how these biases are formed and reinforced in everyday interactions.

Types of Bias and Their Real-World Impact:

Leaders are guided through an in-depth examination of key biases that commonly influence workplace dynamics:

- **Affinity Bias:** The tendency to favor individuals who share similar backgrounds, interests, or experiences. This can lead to hiring or promoting those who "fit in" while overlooking diverse talent.

- **Confirmation Bias:** The inclination to seek information that confirms existing beliefs or stereotypes. For example, interpreting a candidate's minor mistake as evidence of incompetence while ignoring their achievements.
- **Attribution Bias:** The habit of attributing success to external factors for some groups while crediting personal effort for others. This often affects performance evaluations, with certain employees facing harsher scrutiny.

By dissecting these biases, leaders see how they can unknowingly shape decisions in recruitment, promotions, team assignments, and performance reviews. Programs use relatable examples and exercises, such as role-playing scenarios in which leaders analyze and challenge biased behavior, to make these biases more tangible.

Linking Bias to Workplace Inequities

Leaders learn to connect unconscious bias to more considerable systemic challenges within their organizations. They explore how these biases contribute to inequities, such as underrepresentation in leadership roles, wage gaps, and barriers to career advancement for marginalized groups. Through this lens, leaders recognize their role in perpetuating or dismantling these patterns.

Interactive Learning for Lasting Change

To ensure the learning is actionable, programs incorporate interactive elements like group discussions, bias-spotting activities, and self-assessment tools. These methods help leaders reflect on their own behaviors and decisions, fostering a commitment to conscious, inclusive leadership practices.

By understanding the science and impact of unconscious bias, leaders are better equipped to identify and mitigate its influence, creating a more equitable and inclusive workplace culture.

2. Self-Reflection Exercises:

Leadership development programs emphasize self-awareness as the first step in addressing unconscious bias. Participants are guided through carefully designed self-assessment tools that reveal the biases they may unknowingly hold. These assessments often include implicit association tests, which measure automatic associations between concepts (e.g., gender, and leadership) to uncover hidden prejudices.

Reflective exercises complement these tools by encouraging participants to think critically about their past decisions and behaviors. Leaders are prompted to ask themselves questions such as:

- *Have I consistently favored specific individuals or groups in hiring or promotions?*
- *Do I unintentionally judge others based on their background, appearance, or mannerisms?*
- *How do my personal experiences influence the assumptions I make about others?*

Journaling and facilitated discussions often accompany these exercises, allowing participants to process their insights in a supportive environment. This combination of tools helps leaders confront uncomfortable truths and take ownership of their biases.

Real-Life Scenarios and Case Studies for Practical Understanding

To bridge the gap between theory and practice, programs integrate real-life scenarios and case studies that illustrate how unconscious bias manifests in workplace dynamics. These examples are drawn from various industries and organizational contexts, ensuring relevance and relatability.

For instance:

A case study might describe a hiring committee's decision to prioritize "cultural fit," leading to the exclusion of a highly qualified candidate from an underrepresented group. Participants analyze the scenario to identify the biases at play and discuss alternative approaches.

Scenarios could include situations where biases influence performance reviews, such as a manager attributing an employee's success to "luck" rather than skill due to preconceived notions.

Interactive activities, like role-playing or group problem-solving, enable participants to practice recognizing and addressing bias in real-time. These exercises simulate common workplace challenges, giving leaders a safe space to experiment with inclusive decision-making.

Connecting Insights to Leadership Behavior

By exploring their own biases and engaging with real-world examples, leaders develop a deeper understanding of how unconscious bias affects their decision-making processes. They begin to see patterns in their interactions—how biases shape their choices in hiring, promotions, conflict resolution, and team management.

This awareness is transformative, as it empowers leaders to take proactive steps toward more equitable practices. They learn to pause and question their assumptions, seek diverse perspectives, and implement strategies to mitigate bias. Programs also encourage leaders to share their reflections with peers, fostering accountability and collective growth.

By combining self-assessment, reflection, and practical scenarios, these programs equip leaders with the tools they need to recognize and disrupt unconscious bias, paving the way for a more inclusive and equitable workplace.

3. **Practical Strategies for Inclusion**

Effective programs begin with an exploration of how unconscious bias operates at the neurological level. Leaders are introduced to the cognitive processes that drive automatic associations and stereotypes, such as the brain's tendency to categorize information quickly for efficiency. These shortcuts, while natural, often lead to biased judgments and assumptions. Through engaging content—such as neuroscience-based explanations, case studies, and practical examples—leaders gain a deeper understanding of how these biases are formed and reinforced in everyday interactions.

Types of Bias and Their Real-World Impact:

Leaders are guided through an in-depth examination of key biases that commonly influence workplace dynamics:

- **Affinity Bias:** The tendency to favor individuals who share similar backgrounds, interests, or experiences. This can lead to hiring or promoting those who "fit in" while overlooking diverse talent.

- **Confirmation Bias:** The inclination to seek information that confirms existing beliefs or stereotypes. For example, interpreting a candidate's minor mistake as evidence of incompetence while ignoring their achievements.
- **Attribution Bias:** The habit of attributing success to external factors for some groups while crediting personal effort for others. This often affects performance evaluations, with certain employees facing harsher scrutiny.

By dissecting these biases, leaders see how they can unknowingly shape decisions in recruitment, promotions, team assignments, and performance reviews. Programs use relatable examples and exercises, such as role-playing scenarios in which leaders analyze and challenge biased behavior, to make these biases more tangible.

Linking Bias to Workplace Inequities:

Leaders learn to connect unconscious bias to more considerable systemic challenges within their organizations. They explore how these biases contribute to inequities, such as underrepresentation in leadership roles, wage gaps, and barriers to career advancement for marginalized groups. Through this lens, leaders recognize their role in perpetuating or dismantling these patterns.

Interactive Learning for Lasting Change:

To ensure actionable learning, programs incorporate interactive elements like group discussions, bias-spotting activities, and self-assessment tools. These methods help leaders reflect on their behaviors and decisions, fostering a commitment to conscious, inclusive leadership practices.

By understanding the science and impact of unconscious bias, leaders are better equipped to identify and mitigate its influence, creating a more equitable and inclusive workplace culture.

Actionable Steps to Counteract Bias:

Training programs emphasize practical strategies that leaders can implement immediately to minimize the influence of bias in their workplace. These steps go beyond theory, providing tools and frameworks that promote fairness and equity:

Standardizing Evaluation Criteria: Leaders learn to develop clear, objective benchmarks for assessing performance, recruitment, and promotions. By defining and consistently applying criteria, they reduce the risk of subjective judgments skewed by unconscious bias. For example, implementing structured interviews with pre-defined questions ensures all candidates are evaluated on the same basis.

Encouraging Diverse Perspectives: Leaders are trained to actively seek input from individuals with different experiences and viewpoints. This involves creating spaces where team members feel comfortable expressing dissenting opinions and challenging groupthink. Diverse perspectives enhance decision-making and foster innovation as solutions are evaluated from multiple angles.

Interrupting Bias in Real Time: Programs teach leaders to recognize and address bias as it arises. This could mean speaking up when someone is unfairly stereotyped in a meeting or questioning assumptions that influence hiring decisions. Leaders practice using strategies such as pausing discussions to reflect on potential biases or asking clarifying questions to uncover unintentional bias.

Using Inclusive Language:

Language is a powerful tool in shaping workplace culture. Leaders are taught to be intentional with their words, ensuring that their communication reflects respect and inclusivity. This involves:

Avoiding Gendered or Exclusionary Terms: Leaders are encouraged to use gender-neutral terms (e.g., "team" instead of "guys") and to avoid phrases that may exclude or stereotype specific groups.

Recognizing and Respecting Pronouns: Training emphasizes the importance of addressing employees by their preferred pronouns and names, which fosters a sense of belonging and respect.

Adopting Collaborative Language: Leaders learn to use phrases like "we" and "us" to emphasize teamwork and shared goals, reinforcing a sense of unity.

Fostering Valued and Heard Employees:

Inclusive leadership involves creating an environment where all employees feel recognized, appreciated, and empowered to contribute. Training equips leaders with tools to:

- **Actively Listen:** Leaders practice deep listening skills, which involve giving full attention, acknowledging employees' concerns, and responding thoughtfully.
- **Provide Equal Opportunities for Input:** Leaders ensure that everyone has an opportunity to participate in discussions, whether through structured brainstorming sessions or inclusive meeting practices. For instance, they may rotate who leads discussions or ensure quieter team members have a chance to share ideas.
- **Celebrate Contributions:** Recognizing and rewarding employees' unique strengths and accomplishments builds morale and demonstrates that their efforts are valued.

By focusing on these actionable steps and communication practices, leaders are equipped to build a workplace culture that not only reduces bias but actively promotes inclusivity and equity. This commitment inspires trust, improves team dynamics, and positions the organization as a leader in diversity and inclusion.

4. **Role-Playing and Scenario-Based Learning**

Interactive workshops provide a dynamic, hands-on approach to leadership training by simulating real workplace scenarios where biases may arise. These sessions are not just theoretical; they create opportunities for leaders to engage directly with challenges they are likely to encounter in their roles. Through immersive role-playing, leaders experience situations such as team meetings where a minority voice is overlooked or hiring decisions that unconscious preferences may sway. These simulations allow participants to practice recognizing and addressing biases as they emerge in real time, helping them develop the skills needed to respond appropriately in actual work settings.

By participating in these role-playing exercises, leaders build both the competence and confidence to apply the principles of inclusive leadership. As they practice behaviors like encouraging diverse perspectives during decision-making or intervening when biased remarks are made, they begin to internalize these practices. This hands-on approach gives them a chance to explore what inclusive behavior looks like in action and to receive constructive feedback in a supportive environment. Through these workshops, leaders gain valuable experience in navigating the complexities of real-world bias situations, learning not just how to identify bias but how to address it effectively.

Role-playing also encourages leaders to refine their communication skills, particularly in sensitive or challenging interactions. They practice handling difficult conversations, such as addressing microaggressions or providing feedback on biased behavior, in a way that is both assertive and empathetic. This practice helps them feel more comfortable navigating these conversations when they arise in their actual work environment, ensuring they approach every situation with the confidence to foster a more inclusive atmosphere.

Additionally, these workshops create a space for group reflection, allowing leaders to discuss the challenges they faced during the exercises and share insights on how to incorporate inclusive behaviors into their everyday roles. These discussions not only reinforce the learning but also create a collective commitment to inclusivity across teams. By the end of the workshop, leaders walk away with enhanced awareness of their own biases, practical tools to interrupt bias when it occurs, and a stronger sense of accountability to create an equitable workplace.

This approach ensures that the learning is deeply rooted and actionable. Leaders who engage in these interactive workshops are better equipped to foster inclusion, confront bias head-on, and lead with empathy and fairness. As a result, they are more prepared to build work environments where all employees feel valued, heard, and empowered to contribute to the organization's success.

Such training programs are not one-off events; they should be integrated into ongoing leadership development initiatives. Continuous learning ensures that leaders stay aware of evolving challenges and remain committed to creating an inclusive culture.

Promoting Inclusive Leadership Behaviors

Without encouraging inclusive behaviors on a daily basis, training alone is insufficient. To have an impact on the entire business, leaders must act in a way that exemplifies the values of equity and inclusion. Here are some tips for developing inclusive leadership habits:

1. **Modeling Accountability:**

Inclusive leaders understand that leadership is not just about making decisions but about owning those decisions and their outcomes, both good and bad. They lead with a sense of responsibility, recognizing that their actions have a direct impact on their teams, the organization, and its culture. When mistakes occur, inclusive leaders are the first to acknowledge them, demonstrating vulnerability and transparency. Instead of shifting blame or avoiding accountability, they openly admit when something went wrong, take responsibility for their part, and actively seek solutions. This openness not only fosters trust within their teams but also creates a learning culture where mistakes are seen as opportunities for growth, not failures to be hidden.

A key characteristic of inclusive leaders is their willingness to learn from their mistakes and to continually improve. They approach challenges with a growth mindset, seeing each situation as an opportunity to develop new skills, refine their approach, and better serve their teams. They don't just reflect on what went wrong—they seek out feedback, engage in self-reflection, and actively work to adjust their behavior. This continual process of learning not only helps them become better leaders but also sets a powerful example for their teams, showing that no one is ever "done" learning or growing.

By consistently holding themselves accountable, inclusive leaders set a standard for their teams. They demonstrate that accountability is not just a top-down expectation but a shared responsibility. When team members see their leaders take ownership of their actions, they are more likely to adopt the same attitude. Leaders who lead by example create an environment where accountability is valued and where individuals feel empowered to own their actions, speak up when something isn't right, and collaborate in ways that encourage growth and improvement.

This culture of accountability is essential for fostering trust and respect within teams. When everyone, from the top down, is held to the same high standards, it creates a sense of fairness and mutual respect. Team members feel more comfortable taking risks, offering new ideas, and speaking up when they see something that could be improved. In turn, this strengthens the team dynamic, promotes innovation, and ultimately contributes to the organization's success.

Inclusive leaders hold themselves accountable and don't just guide their teams through challenges—they create a culture where responsibility, growth, and collaboration are central to success.

2. Empowering Diverse Voices

Inclusive leaders recognize that the richness of a diverse workforce comes from the varied backgrounds, experiences, and perspectives that each individual brings to the table. They understand that the best solutions and innovations emerge when these diverse viewpoints are actively sought, valued, and integrated into decision-making processes. Rather than relying solely on their insights or the opinions of a select few, inclusive leaders intentionally create opportunities to hear from everyone in their teams. They foster environments where every voice is given equal weight, ensuring that ideas from individuals at all levels and from all backgrounds are considered and respected.

To encourage open dialogue, inclusive leaders establish platforms that make sharing ideas and feedback both accessible and comfortable for all employees. They set up open forums, town hall meetings, or roundtable discussions that go beyond formal meetings, creating spaces for honest and inclusive conversations. These platforms provide a safe space for employees to speak candidly about their thoughts, concerns, and creative suggestions without fear of judgment or retribution. Leaders ensure these forums are welcoming by setting clear expectations that all opinions are valued and that everyone, regardless of rank or role, is encouraged to contribute.

Moreover, inclusive leaders take proactive steps to ensure that louder voices or more assertive personalities do not dominate these discussions. They employ strategies such as moderating the conversation to ensure a balanced exchange or rotating facilitators to ensure that diverse perspectives are consistently highlighted. They may also leverage tools such as anonymous feedback systems to give quieter or more reserved team members a chance to voice their thoughts without feeling exposed. This approach ensures that the conversation remains equitable, with everyone—regardless of their background, tenure, or personality—feeling empowered to speak up and be heard.

Through these efforts, inclusive leaders not only gather a wealth of diverse insights but also create a culture of mutual respect, collaboration, and psychological safety. Employees feel that their contributions matter, which boosts morale, engagement, and a sense of belonging. These leaders know that the more inclusive and open the environment, the more creative and effective their team will be in solving problems, making decisions, and driving success. By fostering a culture where everyone has the opportunity to share their ideas, inclusive leaders pave the way for more innovative, dynamic, and resilient teams.

3. **Practicing Empathy:**

Understanding the unique experiences of employees is a cornerstone of inclusive leadership. Leaders who take the time to truly listen—without judgment or preconceived notions—create an environment where individuals feel safe to express themselves. This kind of listening goes beyond hearing words; it involves actively engaging with the emotions, challenges, and perspectives of each employee. By asking thoughtful, open-ended questions, inclusive leaders show that they genuinely care about understanding the experiences of others. They create a dialogue that invites employees to share their thoughts and concerns, making sure that everyone feels seen and valued. In doing so, leaders foster trust and transparency, which are essential for building a culture of inclusivity and psychological safety.

Moreover, an inclusive leader goes a step further by prioritizing the well-being of employees, recognizing that their emotional and mental health is just as important as their professional contributions. Leaders who show genuine concern for the well-being of their teams actively invest in resources that support their staff, such as mental health programs, flexible work arrangements, and opportunities for professional growth. This demonstrates that inclusivity isn't just about diversity in the workplace but also about ensuring that every employee has the support they need to thrive in both their personal and professional lives.

Empathy is an essential trait for inclusive leadership, as it enables leaders to identify and understand the barriers that marginalized employees often face. Empathetic leaders make it a point to recognize the challenges that individuals from underrepresented groups experience—whether it's bias in performance reviews, lack of career advancement opportunities, or cultural insensitivity in the workplace. By acknowledging these barriers, leaders can begin to address systemic issues that may otherwise go unnoticed. Empathy helps leaders to step into their employees' shoes, seeing the world from their perspective and understanding the real-world implications of their experiences.

Furthermore, empathetic leadership isn't just about recognizing problems; it's about actively working to remove those obstacles. Inclusive leaders are committed to advocating for policies, processes, and changes that eliminate the barriers faced by marginalized groups. This might mean implementing training to reduce bias in recruitment, creating mentorship opportunities for underrepresented employees, or ensuring equitable access to career development programs. By taking action to remove these barriers, empathetic leaders help to level the playing field and ensure that all employees have the opportunity to succeed and grow within the organization.

Ultimately, understanding and empathy go hand-in-hand in creating an inclusive leadership style that benefits everyone. When leaders listen deeply, ask the right questions, and respond with compassion and action, they not only foster an environment of trust and respect but also drive meaningful change. This approach empowers employees to reach their full potential, ensuring that the workplace is not just diverse but genuinely inclusive.

4. **Challenging the Status Quo:**

Inclusive leaders actively challenge the traditional norms and systems that have historically reinforced inequality. Rather than accepting outdated practices as the status quo, they recognize that these norms can subtly perpetuate biases and exclude diverse voices. These leaders engage in a continuous process of questioning and evaluating existing structures within their organizations, from recruitment practices to team dynamics, with a keen eye on how they may inadvertently favor certain groups over others. Their willingness to examine these ingrained practices is not only an acknowledgment of past inequities but also a commitment to shaping a more inclusive and equitable future.

By questioning these traditional norms, inclusive leaders become powerful advocates for change, pushing for structural reforms that ensure fairer outcomes for all employees. One of the most significant steps they take is advocating for blind recruitment practices, which remove identifying information—such as names, genders, and educational backgrounds—from job applications. This helps to eliminate bias from the hiring process, ensuring that candidates are evaluated based on their skills, experience, and qualifications alone, rather than being influenced by unconscious biases related to their identity or background. In doing so, inclusive leaders level the playing field, providing equal opportunities for talent from diverse backgrounds.

Beyond recruitment, inclusive leaders understand that access to growth opportunities is just as crucial in fostering an equitable environment. They champion policies and practices that ensure all employees, regardless of their background or identity, have an equal opportunity to advance within the organization. This includes advocating for mentorship programs that specifically support underrepresented groups, ensuring transparent promotion processes, and creating pathways for skill development that are accessible to everyone. By making sure these opportunities are not reserved for a select few, they foster a culture of meritocracy where individuals are recognized for their contributions and potential rather than their demographics.

Inclusive leaders also push for the ongoing evaluation and rethinking of organizational processes that may unconsciously reinforce inequities. They challenge their teams and organizations to be more than just compliant with diversity and inclusion goals but to actively build systems and cultures that support long-term structural change. Through their leadership, they create an environment where outdated norms do not limit innovation, talent, and opportunities but are instead fueled by the diverse and dynamic contributions of all employees. In this way, they set a foundation for organizations that thrive on inclusivity, equity, and fairness—ultimately leading to a more substantial, more diverse workplace where everyone can succeed.

5. **Fostering Collaboration:**

Leaders who emphasize shared goals and value each team member's contribution create a collaborative environment where everyone feels appreciated. By highlighting how individual efforts align with the team's mission, they foster unity and drive success. When conflicts arise, effective leaders mediate with fairness, ensuring all voices are heard and resolving issues constructively. They set clear expectations for respectful behavior, promoting inclusivity and openness. This approach strengthens team dynamics, builds trust, and encourages creativity, helping the team work cohesively towards common objectives.

6. **Celebrating Diversity:**

Inclusive leaders don't just tolerate differences—they celebrate them as key drivers of success. By highlighting and rewarding contributions from underrepresented groups, they show that diversity is essential for innovation and growth. These leaders create opportunities for diverse voices to be heard, fostering a sense of belonging and motivating employees to bring their authentic selves to work. By advocating for diversity at every level, inclusive leaders strengthen the organization and ensure that everyone feels valued and empowered to contribute.

7. **Mentoring and Sponsoring Underrepresented Talent:**

Leaders who take an active role in mentoring individuals from underrepresented groups provide essential guidance and support to help them navigate their careers and overcome the unique barriers they often face. By offering mentorship, these leaders create a safe and nurturing environment where mentees can discuss challenges, seek advice, and gain insights into the skills and strategies needed to succeed. This relationship goes beyond traditional guidance, as mentors actively invest in their mentees' growth, offering valuable feedback, networking opportunities, and the encouragement needed to build confidence and resilience. Through consistent support, mentors help mentees identify and develop their strengths, ultimately empowering them to take charge of their career paths.

Sponsorship, however, goes one step further by advocating for these individuals in decision-making spaces, ensuring they are not only seen but also given the recognition and opportunities they deserve. While mentorship focuses on personal and professional development, sponsorship is about opening doors and actively creating pathways to success. Leaders who sponsor underrepresented employees speak up for them in key meetings, nominate them for promotions, and ensure that their contributions are acknowledged in high-level discussions. This advocacy helps break down systemic barriers, ensuring that talented individuals from diverse backgrounds have a seat at the table and are given the same opportunities to advance as their counterparts.

Together, mentoring and sponsorship work to create a more inclusive and equitable workplace. By offering mentorship, leaders help individuals from underrepresented groups build the skills and confidence to excel. Through sponsorship, they provide the advocacy and visibility needed to ensure that these individuals are recognized, celebrated, and given the opportunities they have earned. This dual approach not only empowers individuals but also fosters a culture where talent is nurtured, and diversity is truly valued.

The Ripple Effect of Inclusive Leadership

When leaders develop inclusive mindsets and behaviors, they inspire teams to follow suit. An inclusive leader can transform workplace culture, breaking down silos, boosting morale, and driving innovation. Employees are more likely to feel engaged and committed when they see their leaders championing diversity and equity.

Organizations that prioritize leadership development for inclusion ultimately see tangible benefits: improved employee satisfaction, increased retention of top talent, and enhanced reputation in the market. In a world where inclusivity is not just a moral imperative but a business advantage, leaders have the responsibility—and the opportunity—to pave the way for a better, more equitable future.

By equipping leaders with the knowledge, skills, and behaviors to embrace inclusion, organizations can create workplaces where everyone has a fair shot at success and feels like they belong.

BUILDING A DIVERSE TALENT PIPELINE

A diverse talent pipeline is more than a goal—it reflects an organization's commitment to equity and innovation. It's about creating opportunities for individuals from all backgrounds to bring their unique skills and perspectives to the table. To build this pipeline, organizations must rethink their approach to recruitment and development, ensuring every step foster inclusivity and breaks down barriers.

The journey begins with redefining how talent is sought. Traditional job descriptions often act as gatekeepers, laden with unnecessary qualifications that exclude capable candidates. Instead, focusing on the core skills and competencies required for success can open the door to a broader range of applicants. Simultaneously, expanding recruitment efforts to reach historically underrepresented groups is essential. Partnering with diverse institutions and communities helps organizations connect with individuals who bring fresh perspectives and new ideas.

Once individuals enter the organization, the real work begins. Diversity is not achieved merely by hiring—it must be nurtured through ongoing development. Structured training programs and leadership development initiatives ensure that diverse employees have the tools and support needed to thrive. This requires organizations to go beyond generic professional development and consider the unique challenges that underrepresented employees might face in their career journeys.

Creating an inclusive environment also means addressing the subtle dynamics that can hinder equity. Networking opportunities, often informal and exclusive, need to be reimagined as accessible and intentional spaces where everyone can build meaningful connections. Employee resource groups can provide a platform for underrepresented employees to find support and share experiences while also serving as a valuable resource for leadership to understand the nuances of workplace inclusivity.

Humanizing these efforts is critical. Building a diverse talent pipeline isn't about ticking boxes or meeting quotas—it's about transforming lives and creating lasting change. Imagine a talented individual who, through support and development, rises from feeling overlooked to becoming a confident leader. That transformation isn't just their victory—it's a win for the organization, which gains a dedicated, innovative contributor.

By embedding these practices into the fabric of workplace culture, organizations can move beyond simply recruiting for diversity. They can cultivate a thriving, inclusive environment where every individual is empowered to succeed and contribute to a shared vision. When diversity becomes an integral part of talent development, it transforms organizations into dynamic spaces where change is not only embraced but celebrated.

The Role of Mentorship and Sponsorship

Mentorship and sponsorship play critical roles in advancing underrepresented groups and fostering diversity within an organization. While both are essential, they serve distinct purposes in supporting talent development.

Mentorship provides guidance and advice, helping individuals navigate challenges and develop professionally. A mentor might share career insights, offer constructive feedback, and serve as a sounding board for personal and professional growth. Formal mentorship programs ensure that underrepresented employees have access to this kind of support, creating a structured pathway for them to learn and thrive within the organization.

Sponsorship, on the other hand, goes beyond guidance. Sponsors use their influence and networks to actively advocate for their protégés, recommending them for high-profile projects, promotions, or leadership roles. This advocacy is particularly crucial for employees who might otherwise be overlooked in decision-making processes. Sponsorship programs encourage leaders to identify emerging talent and champion their growth, ensuring that diverse employees are not just included but given the chance to lead.

By fostering both mentorship and sponsorship, organizations create a dynamic support system where employees not only feel seen but are empowered to rise to their full potential. These relationships can have a transformative impact, breaking down barriers and building a culture of equity and inclusion.

LEGAL AND ETHICAL CONSIDERATIONS

Navigating the legal and ethical context becomes crucial as businesses attempt to establish inclusive and diverse workplaces. Errors can have serious repercussions, including fines and harm to one's reputation.

Understanding Laws and Regulations Related to Bias and Diversity

Initiatives for workplace diversity and inclusion (D&I) benefit businesses and are required by law. Around the world, a number of laws and regulations safeguard workers from discrimination and encourage fair treatment. Comprehending these rules guarantees adherence and shows a dedication to justice.

Key Legal Frameworks in Major Regions:

United States:

The United States has implemented several landmark laws to foster equitable workplaces and prevent discrimination. These laws set the foundation for diversity, equity, and inclusion (DEI) efforts, ensuring that all employees are treated with dignity and fairness.

Title VII of the Civil Rights Act (1964)

What It Does:

This cornerstone legislation prohibits workplace discrimination based on race, color, religion, sex, or national origin. Title VII applies to employers with 15 or more employees and covers all aspects of employment, including hiring, promotions, compensation, and termination.

Why It Matters:

Before Title VII, discrimination in hiring and workplace policies was widespread and unchecked. This act provided a legal recourse for marginalized groups to challenge inequities, promoting a more level playing field in employment.

Key Features:

Prohibits harassment based on protected characteristics, such as racial slurs or inappropriate jokes.

Requires employers to provide reasonable accommodations for employees' religious practices, as long as it doesn't cause undue hardship to the business.

Protects against retaliation for employees who file complaints or participate in investigations regarding discrimination.

Modern Applications:

Gender identity and sexual orientation are now recognized under the "sex" category, thanks to Supreme Court rulings, making Title VII even more inclusive.

Employers must conduct bias training to prevent implicit discrimination that could lead to violations.

Americans with Disabilities Act (ADA)

What It Does:

Enacted in 1990, the ADA requires employers to provide reasonable accommodations for employees with disabilities, ensuring they have equal access to employment opportunities. It also prohibits discrimination against individuals with physical or mental impairments.

Why It Matters:

The ADA was a groundbreaking step toward workplace inclusion for people with disabilities. Removing physical, technological, and procedural barriers opened doors for millions of qualified workers previously overlooked.

Key Features:

Employers must modify workspaces or processes to accommodate employees with disabilities (e.g., installing ramps, providing assistive technology, or altering work schedules).

Covers a broad range of disabilities, including chronic illnesses, mobility impairments, mental health conditions, and learning disabilities.

Protects employees from discrimination during hiring, job assignments, promotions, and terminations.

Modern Applications:

The rise of remote work has created new opportunities for ADA compliance, such as providing flexible work options for employees with mobility or mental health challenges.

Technology companies are increasingly designing accessible tools and software to meet ADA standards.

Equal Pay Act (1963)

What It Does:

This law mandates that men and women performing substantially equal work under similar conditions must receive equal pay. The Equal Pay Act addresses wage disparities based on gender and requires that job roles be evaluated based on skill, effort, and responsibility.

Why It Matters:

When the law was passed, women earned significantly less than men for performing the same jobs. The Equal Pay Act challenged this systemic inequity, paving the way for fairer compensation practices.

Key Features:

- Prohibits employers from justifying pay disparities based on gender alone.
- Allows pay differences only when based on factors like seniority, merit, or measurable productivity.
- Covers wages, benefits, bonuses, and other forms of compensation.

Modern Applications:

Transparency in pay practices has become a critical focus, with organizations publishing gender pay gap reports to ensure compliance.

Advocacy for intersectional equity addresses pay disparities that disproportionately affect women of color and other marginalized groups.

Why These Laws Matter Today

While these laws were enacted decades ago, their principles remain as relevant as ever. They provide the legal framework to hold organizations accountable, ensure fair treatment, and protect the rights of employees. However, compliance alone is not enough. Employers must go beyond legal obligations by fostering a culture that values diversity, equity, and inclusion.

By embracing these laws as part of a broader ethical commitment, organizations can avoid legal pitfalls and unlock the benefits of a truly inclusive workplace.

1. **European Union:**

The European Union (EU) has established robust laws and directives aimed at promoting equality and fairness across its member states. These regulations not only prohibit discrimination but also encourage ethical practices in handling sensitive information, creating a foundation for inclusive workplaces across Europe.

Equality Directives

What They Do:

The EU enforces a series of Equality Directives designed to combat discrimination based on age, disability, sexual orientation, religion, race, and gender. These directives aim to harmonize anti-discrimination laws across all member states, ensuring that individuals enjoy equal rights and opportunities regardless of their background or identity.

Key Directives Include:

The Employment Equality Framework Directive (2000/78/EC) prohibits workplace discrimination based on age, disability, sexual orientation, and religion or belief.

The Race Equality Directive (2000/43/EC) Prohibits discrimination based on race or ethnicity in employment, education, healthcare, and access to goods and services.

The Gender Equality Directives Cover equal treatment for men and women, particularly in employment and access to social protections.

Why They Matter:

These directives form the backbone of workplace equality across the EU. They provide a legal basis for employees to challenge discriminatory practices and hold organizations accountable. Beyond compliance, they push companies to embrace inclusivity as a competitive advantage.

Modern Applications:

- Age and Disability: Employers are required to provide reasonable accommodations and prevent ageism in hiring and promotions.
- Sexual Orientation and Religion: Companies are developing policies to ensure LGBTQ+ inclusivity and respect for religious practices.
- Intersectionality: Organizations are increasingly recognizing the need to address overlapping identities, such as the challenges

faced by women of color or older employees with disabilities.

General Data Protection Regulation (GDPR)

What It Does:

GDPR, primarily known as a data privacy law, governs the collection, storage, and use of personal data within the EU. While its primary focus is on protecting individuals' privacy, GDPR has significant implications for handling diversity-related data in ethical and non-discriminatory ways.

Why It Matters:

Diversity, equity, and inclusion (DEI) initiatives often require the collection and analysis of sensitive demographic data, such as race, gender, or disability status. GDPR ensures that this data is handled responsibly, safeguarding the privacy of employees while enabling organizations to track and improve their DEI efforts.

Key Provisions Relevant to DEI:

- **Consent:** Organizations must obtain explicit consent before collecting sensitive data, ensuring employees understand why their information is being gathered and how it will be used.

- **Purpose Limitation:** Data can only be collected for specified, legitimate purposes, such as monitoring diversity metrics or ensuring compliance with equality laws.
- **Data Minimization:** Only data necessary for achieving the stated purpose should be collected, reducing the risk of misuse or breaches.
- **Anonymization:** Sensitive data must be anonymized or pseudonymized to protect individuals' identities.

Ethical Implications:

Organizations must ensure transparency in how they collect and use diversity-related data, fostering trust among employees.

Misuse or unauthorized sharing of data could result in legal penalties and erode workplace morale and trust.

Ethical DEI programs should balance the need for data-driven insights with employees' right to privacy.

Modern Applications:

- **Diversity Audits:** GDPR-compliant tools are being used to conduct audits that identify gaps in representation without compromising individual privacy.
- **Bias-Free Recruitment:** Companies are using anonymized data to reduce bias in hiring decisions, such as removing names or photos from resumes.
- **Global Compliance:** Multinational organizations operating in the EU are aligning their practices with GDPR while also addressing region-specific DEI challenges.

Why These Frameworks Are Crucial for Progress

The Equality Directives and GDPR exemplify how legal frameworks can drive meaningful change in workplaces. By addressing discrimination and promoting ethical data practices, they empower organizations to build fairer, more inclusive environments. However, compliance should be seen as the starting point, not the finish line. Employers must go beyond the letter of the law to create cultures where equality and respect are deeply embedded in everyday practices.

When implemented thoughtfully, these regulations enable organizations to harness the full potential of their workforce while maintaining ethical integrity, ensuring that progress in diversity and inclusion is both measurable and sustainable.

2. United Kingdom:

The Equality Act 2010 is a landmark piece of legislation in the United Kingdom designed to protect individuals from discrimination and ensure equal opportunities for all, regardless of their background. It consolidates previous anti-discrimination laws into a single, cohesive framework, making it easier for individuals and organizations to understand their rights and responsibilities.

Understanding the Core Principles of the Equality Act 2010

At its heart, the Equality Act aims to foster an inclusive and fair society. In the workplace, this means ensuring that no one is disadvantaged or mistreated due to characteristics they cannot change or should not be penalized for. These are legally defined as protected characteristics and include:

- Age
- Disability
- Gender reassignment
- Marriage and civil partnership
- Pregnancy and maternity
- Race
- Religion or belief
- Sex
- Sexual orientation

By addressing these characteristics, the Act seeks to create an environment where everyone can thrive professionally, free from bias or prejudice.

Key Features of the Equality Act in the Workplace

- Protection Against Discrimination
- The Act prohibits various forms of discrimination, including:
- **Direct Discrimination:** Treating someone less favorably due to a protected characteristic.

Example: Rejecting a qualified candidate because of their race or gender.
- **Indirect Discrimination:** Policies or practices that appear neutral but disproportionately disadvantage certain groups. *Example*: Requiring all employees to work late, which might unfairly impact those with caregiving responsibilities.
- **Harassment:** Unwanted behavior related to a protected characteristic that creates an intimidating or hostile environment. *Example*: Making inappropriate jokes about someone's disability.
- **Victimization:** Mistreating someone because they've made or supported a complaint under the Act. *Example*: Denying promotion to an employee who filed a grievance about workplace discrimination.

Reasonable Adjustments

Employers are required to make reasonable adjustments to accommodate individuals with disabilities.

Example: Installing ramps for wheelchair access, providing screen readers for visually impaired employees, or offering flexible working hours for mental health management.

Equal Pay and Gender Pay Gap Transparency

The Act enforces the principle of equal pay for equal work, ensuring that men and women receive the same remuneration for similar roles. Large organizations are also mandated to report their gender pay gaps, fostering accountability and promoting pay equity.

Positive Action

Employers are encouraged to take positive action to address the underrepresentation or disadvantage faced by certain groups.

Example: Offering leadership training programs targeted at women in male-dominated industries.

The Equality Act in Practice: Benefits for Employees and Employers

For Employees:

The Equality Act provides a robust safety net, ensuring individuals can report discriminatory practices without fear of retaliation. It empowers employees to seek fairness and promotes a sense of belonging within the workplace.

For Employers:

Organizations that embrace the principles of the Equality Act gain significant advantages:

- **Enhanced Reputation:** Inclusive workplaces attract top talent and foster loyalty among employees.
- **Increased Innovation:** Diverse teams bring varied perspectives, driving creativity and problem-solving.
- **Legal Compliance:** Adhering to the Act minimizes the risk of costly lawsuits and reputational damage.

Challenges and Opportunities in Implementing the Equality Act

While the Act provides a clear framework, implementation can be complex. Organizations often face challenges such as:

- **Unconscious Bias:** Training and awareness campaigns are crucial to addressing ingrained stereotypes.
- **Resistance to Change:** Transparent communication and leadership buy-in are vital to overcoming pushback.
- **Monitoring and Evaluation:** Regular audits and employee feedback ensure policies remain practical and relevant.

However, these challenges present opportunities for growth. Employers who invest in inclusive practices often see measurable improvements in employee engagement, retention, and productivity.

3. **Global Standards:**

The International Labour Organization (ILO) has been a global champion for workers' rights since its founding in 1919. Among its many contributions, the ILO has established conventions that set a universal benchmark for eliminating discrimination in employment and ensuring equal opportunities for all. These conventions are not just documents—they represent a commitment to human dignity, fairness, and inclusion.

Key ILO Conventions Addressing Discrimination

Convention No. 111: Discrimination (Employment and Occupation) Convention, 1958

This convention is a cornerstone in the fight against workplace discrimination. It defines discrimination as any distinction, exclusion, or preference based on race, color, sex, religion, political opinion, national extraction, or social origin that nullifies or impairs equality of opportunity or treatment.

Countries ratifying this convention are required to take proactive measures to promote equality, ensure equitable access to employment, and eliminate systemic barriers. This is not just about legal compliance—it's about creating workplaces where everyone feels valued and can thrive.

Convention No. 100: Equal Remuneration Convention, 1951

This convention focuses on wage equality, advocating for equal pay for work of equal value regardless of gender. It challenges the historical pay gap between men and women and encourages employers to adopt transparent and fair compensation practices.

The principles of these conventions are more relevant than ever in today's world. Organizations that embrace them are better equipped to attract diverse talent, foster innovation, and enhance employee loyalty.

Why ILO Conventions Matter

Adhering to ILO standards is not just about legal obligations—it's a reflection of ethical leadership. These conventions:

- Set a moral compass for businesses and governments.
- Provide a roadmap for creating equitable workplace policies.
- Serve as a global benchmark for justice and human rights.

Real-World Impact

Consider a multinational corporation with offices in several countries. By aligning its policies with ILO conventions, the company can create a unified approach to diversity and inclusion, ensuring that all employees, regardless of location, have access to the same opportunities and protections.

UN Sustainable Development Goals: Reducing Inequalities Through Goal 10

The United Nations' Sustainable Development Goals (SDGs) are a blueprint for global progress, addressing issues ranging from poverty to climate change. Goal 10: Reduced Inequalities stands out as a clarion call for fairness in all aspects of society, including the workplace.

Understanding Goal 10

Goal 10 emphasizes reducing inequality within and among countries. While the scope of this goal is broad, its principles are deeply intertwined with workplace equality. Key targets under Goal 10 include:

Empowering and promoting the social, economic, and political inclusion of all, irrespective of age, gender, disability, race, ethnicity, origin, religion, or economic status.

Ensuring equal opportunity and reducing income disparities.

Adopting policies, especially fiscal and social protections, to promote greater equality.

What Goal 10 Means for Workplaces

In practical terms, Goal 10 challenges organizations to:

- **Diversify Leadership:** Ensure that leadership teams reflect the diversity of the workforce. Representation matters—it inspires employees and strengthens decision-making.
- **Close Wage Gaps:** Address inequities in pay by conducting regular audits and implementing transparent salary structures.
- **Foster Inclusive Practices:** Provide equal access to training, promotions, and leadership opportunities.

The Workplace as a Catalyst for Change

The workplace is a microcosm of society. By embedding the principles of Goal 10 into organizational practices, businesses can drive meaningful change. For instance:

A company that prioritizes hiring from underrepresented communities not only benefits from diverse perspectives but also helps to reduce societal inequalities.

Equitable maternity and paternity leave policies promote gender equality at work and home.

A Collective Responsibility

Achieving Goal 10 requires collective action. Governments must enforce anti-discrimination laws, organizations must lead by example, and individuals must challenge biases. Together, we can create workplaces that not only reflect but also drive societal progress.

The Interplay Between ILO Conventions and Goal 10

The ILO conventions and UN SDG Goal 10 are not isolated frameworks—they complement and reinforce each other. Both emphasize the importance of inclusion, equity, and respect for human rights.

ILO conventions provide the regulatory framework, ensuring that workplaces meet a minimum standard of fairness.

Goal 10 broadens the perspective, encouraging organizations to go beyond compliance and actively promote equity and inclusion.

By integrating these principles into workplace policies and practices, organizations can build a foundation for sustainable success. After all, when employees feel respected and valued, they bring their best selves to work—benefiting individuals, organizations, and society as a whole.

In embracing the spirit of the ILO conventions and Goal 10, organizations can transform themselves into forces for good, championing a future where opportunity and dignity are the rights of all, not the privilege of a few. The question is not whether we can afford to prioritize equality but whether we can afford not to.

Common Legal Risks to Avoid:

- Discriminatory Hiring Practices: Ensure job descriptions and interview processes are free from bias.
- Retaliation: Protect employees who report discrimination or advocate for inclusivity.

- Unintentional Bias in AI Tools: Regularly audit algorithms used in hiring or promotion decisions to ensure fairness.

Practical Steps for Compliance:

- Conduct regular legal audits to align with changing regulations.
- Train HR and leadership teams on anti-discrimination laws and inclusive practices.
- Maintain precise, accessible reporting mechanisms for grievances.

Ensuring Ethical Practices in DEI Efforts

While legal compliance provides a baseline, ethics elevate diversity, equity, and inclusion (DEI) efforts to foster genuine change. Ethical practices ensure that DEI initiatives are not just about checking boxes but about building trust and respect among employees.

Principles of Ethical DEI Practices:

- **Transparency:** Be open about DEI goals, strategies, and challenges. Share progress reports, even if they highlight areas for improvement. Transparency builds trust and accountability.

- **Authenticity:** Avoid performative actions that lack substance. Employees quickly recognize when initiatives are more about appearances than impact. Genuine efforts resonate more deeply.
- **Fairness:** Ensure equitable treatment for all employees. For example, mentoring programs should be accessible to everyone, not just specific groups.
- **Privacy and Respect:** When collecting data related to DEI, such as demographics or employee experiences, handle it with care. Ensure confidentiality and use the data solely to inform positive changes.

Ethical Challenges and Solutions:

Tokenism:

Challenge: Appointing individuals from underrepresented groups as symbolic gestures without meaningful inclusion.

Solution: Provide equal opportunities for career growth and decision-making roles.

Implicit Bias in Leadership:

Challenge: Leaders unconsciously favor certain employees, perpetuating inequities.

Solution: Offer bias training and implement objective evaluation criteria.

Balancing Metrics with Humanity:

Challenge: Focusing solely on numerical diversity targets can dehumanize employees.

Solution: Prioritize qualitative outcomes like employee satisfaction and sense of belonging.

Real-World Examples of Legal and Ethical Leadership

- Starbucks: After an incident of racial profiling in one of its stores, Starbucks took swift action. The company closed thousands of locations for racial bias training and committed to fostering a culture of inclusion.
- Google: Google regularly publishes detailed DEI reports outlining representation data and areas for improvement. This level of transparency reinforces its commitment to ethical practices.
- Patagonia: Known for its ethical practices, Patagonia integrates DEI into its business ethos,

ensuring inclusivity in its workforce and supply chain.

Legal compliance is a crucial foundation for tackling bias and promoting diversity, but ethical practices are what transform workplaces into genuinely inclusive environments. By understanding the laws that govern workplace equity and embedding ethical principles into DEI strategies, organizations can build cultures where everyone feels valued, respected, and empowered to thrive.

Change begins with intention, grows through action, and endures with integrity. As leaders and organizations commit to these principles, they not only comply with legal mandates but also champion the moral imperative of fairness and equality.

PART VI: OVERCOMING ORGANIZATIONAL CHALLENGES

Resistance to change is an inevitable part of any organization's growth journey. It stems from a variety of factors—fear of the unknown, comfort with the status quo, or even fatigue from too many changes happening in rapid succession. Employees may question how a new initiative will impact their job security, their ability to adapt, or their role within the organization. These feelings are natural and valid. Often, resistance isn't just about the change itself; it's a response to the uncertainty and disruption that come with it.

Addressing resistance requires understanding its root causes. For some, skepticism arises from a lack of trust in leadership. If previous changes were poorly implemented or failed to deliver promised results, it's only natural for employees to approach new initiatives with caution. Others may resist simply because they don't see the necessity for change. "If it isn't broken, why fix it?" can feel like a reasonable argument when routines are comfortable and familiar.

The solution lies in creating a culture of open communication and inclusion. Change efforts flourish when leaders take the time to explain the "why" behind their decisions. Employees need to understand how the proposed changes align with the organization's broader goals and how they will benefit not only the company but also individual team members. Leaders must go beyond surface-level explanations and connect the change to a compelling vision of the future—one that inspires hope rather than fear.

One of the most effective ways to combat resistance is to involve employees in the process. People are more likely to support what they help create. When employees have a voice in shaping new initiatives, they feel a sense of ownership that fosters engagement. Whether it's through brainstorming sessions, pilot programs, or feedback opportunities, participation transforms skepticism into collaboration.

Leadership plays a critical role in setting the tone for how change is perceived. Employees watch their leaders closely, looking for signs of authenticity and commitment. When leaders model the behaviors they expect from their teams, it sends a powerful message. A leader who embraces new systems, admits to mistakes and demonstrates a willingness to learn sets an example that encourages others to follow suit.

Empathy is another cornerstone of navigating resistance. Employees need to know their concerns are heard and validated. Change can be overwhelming, and the ability to listen—truly listen—can make all the difference. Addressing fears and frustrations, head-on shows employees that their input matters, fostering trust and reducing pushback.

As the organization moves through the process, celebrating milestones is essential. Recognizing small wins helps build momentum and reminds everyone of the progress being made. It also reinforces the idea that their efforts are making a tangible difference.

Ultimately, overcoming resistance to change isn't about forcing compliance or silencing dissent. It's about leading with empathy, clarity, and patience. By involving employees, maintaining open communication, and demonstrating a commitment to shared success, organizations can transform resistance into resilience. Change may always bring challenges, but with the right approach, it can also unlock new opportunities for growth, innovation, and connection.

ALIGNING DEI WITH ORGANIZATIONAL CULTURE

Diversity, equity, and inclusion (DEI) cannot thrive as standalone initiatives; they must become integral to an organization's culture. When DEI is seamlessly woven into the fabric of everyday business operations, it transforms from being a mere checklist item into a defining aspect of how the organization operates, grows, and thrives.

How to Ensure DEI Becomes Ingrained in the Company's Culture

1. Define Clear DEI Values and Embed Them into the Mission Statement

For DEI to resonate, it must be reflected in the organization's core values and mission. Clearly articulating the importance of diversity, equity, and inclusion sends a powerful message: these are not optional ideals but fundamental principles guiding decision-making, strategy, and behavior.

Example: A company mission might state, *"We celebrate diverse perspectives and strive for equity in all we do to foster an environment where everyone* *belongs."* Such statements set the tone for a DEI-focused culture.

2. Lead by Example at All Levels

Leadership commitment is critical. When executives, managers, and team leaders actively champion DEI principles, their behaviors set a standard. Leaders should consistently demonstrate inclusivity through their actions, whether by amplifying underrepresented voices, addressing inequities, or fostering open dialogue about diversity.

Actionable Tip: Introduce DEI goals into leadership performance metrics to hold leaders accountable for building inclusive teams and equitable policies.

3. Align DEI with Policies and Processes

To indeed weave Diversity, Equity, and Inclusion (DEI) into an organization's culture, these principles must move beyond isolated initiatives and into the heart of daily operations. It begins with rethinking how teams are formed and how opportunities are offered. The hiring process, for example, should reflect inclusivity at every stage, from crafting job postings that invite diverse talent to structuring interview panels that minimize bias. A deliberate and thoughtful approach ensures that every candidate, regardless of their background, feels they have an equal opportunity to contribute and succeed.

Training plays a pivotal role in building awareness and fostering inclusivity across the organization. It's not just about attending a single seminar but about cultivating a continuous learning environment where employees are equipped to recognize and challenge their biases. Through engaging, interactive sessions, employees learn how their behaviors and decisions impact their peers and the broader workplace environment. This ongoing education empowers them to take ownership of creating a more equitable space for everyone.

Performance evaluations are another critical area where DEI must be embedded. When inclusivity becomes part of the success criteria, it sends a strong message that fostering equity and respect is just as important as meeting technical goals. By recognizing and rewarding inclusive behaviors, organizations create a ripple effect, motivating employees and leaders alike to embody these values.

Ultimately, embedding DEI into daily operations means transforming it into a living, breathing part of the organizational culture. It's no longer something that sits on the sidelines or is addressed only in moments of crisis. Instead, it becomes the foundation upon which the organization thrives—a framework that not only shapes policies but also influences the way people interact, collaborate, and grow together. When done right, DEI becomes not just an initiative but a shared ethos, driving long-term success and innovation.

4. Normalize Open Conversations about DEI

Building a culture of transparency is key to fostering diversity and equity. Employees should feel safe discussing these issues without fear of judgment or retaliation. Regular forums, workshops, and anonymous feedback channels create opportunities for open dialogue and continuous improvement. Leadership must actively listen, acknowledge challenges, and act on concerns, demonstrating a commitment to change. Transparency builds trust, ensuring every voice is valued and creating a workplace where inclusion and innovation thrive.

5. Celebrate Wins and Share Stories

Celebrating and highlighting DEI successes is a powerful way to reinforce its importance and inspire ongoing commitment across the organization. When a company implements a new inclusive policy, makes a diverse hire, or achieves more significant equity in promotions, these milestones serve as tangible proof that DEI initiatives are making a real impact. Sharing these achievements not only validates the organization's efforts but also motivates employees to actively contribute to the collective goal of fostering inclusion.

Personal stories from employees add a human touch, transforming abstract initiatives into relatable, lived experiences. When team members share how they've grown, felt a deeper sense of belonging, or been empowered by the organization's focus on diversity, the value of DEI comes to life. These narratives remind everyone that DEI isn't just about statistics or policies—it's about creating an environment where individuals can thrive.

Highlighting such moments can take many forms, from internal newsletters and social media posts to town hall shout-outs or dedicated video stories. The key is to make these successes visible and accessible to all employees. When people see their peers' achievements celebrated, it fosters a sense of pride, reinforces the organization's values, and keeps the momentum alive.

Moreover, celebrating these successes helps maintain accountability. Regularly showcasing progress ensures that DEI remains a priority, not just a one-time effort. It also opens the door for continued reflection and improvement, as it encourages employees and leaders alike to recognize areas where further work is needed.

Ultimately, celebrating and sharing DEI wins creates a ripple effect. It fosters an inclusive culture where progress is acknowledged, stories are shared, and every employee feels part of the journey toward equity and belonging.

The Role of Cultural Ambassadors in Driving Change

Cultural ambassadors make DEI's vision a reality within the organization while leadership establishes it. These ambassadors are staff members who are dedicated to creating a fair and inclusive workplace and are enthusiastic about diversity and inclusion.

1. What Are Cultural Ambassadors?22

Cultural ambassadors are key champions of Diversity, Equity, and Inclusion (DEI) within an organization. These individuals, drawn from all levels and departments, play a unique and transformative role in bridging the gap between leadership's strategic DEI initiatives and the daily experiences of employees. By serving as advocates for inclusivity, they ensure that DEI efforts are not just policies on paper but living principles that resonate throughout the company.

These ambassadors bring the organization's DEI vision to life in practical and relatable ways. Because they come from diverse backgrounds and roles, they have firsthand knowledge of the unique challenges and dynamics within their teams. This perspective allows them to identify areas where DEI strategies can be tailored for maximum impact. For example, they might highlight specific needs in recruitment practices for their department or advocate for adjustments in team dynamics to foster inclusivity.

One of the most vital roles cultural ambassadors play is fostering open communication. They act as trusted confidants and sounding boards for their peers, creating a safe space where employees can share concerns, feedback, and ideas. By channeling this information to leadership, they help ensure that the voices of all employees—especially those who might otherwise go unheard—are included in decision-making processes.

Cultural ambassadors are advocates and educators. They help demystify DEI concepts, breaking them down into actionable behaviors that employees can adopt in their daily work. Through peer-led training sessions, informal discussions, or even one-on-one mentoring, they model inclusive practices and inspire others to do the same.

Leadership support is critical to the success of cultural ambassadors. By empowering these individuals with training, resources, and recognition, organizations can amplify their influence. When employees see their peers actively engaged in driving change, it reinforces the message that DEI is a shared responsibility and integral to the company's culture.

Ultimately, cultural ambassadors act as catalysts for transformation. Their ability to connect, inspire, and advocate ensures that DEI is woven into the fabric of the organization, creating an environment where every employee feels valued, respected, and included.

2. Responsibilities of Cultural Ambassadors

- **Promoting Awareness:** Ambassadors educate their peers about DEI initiatives, resources, and goals.

- **Encouraging Engagement:** By modeling inclusive behaviors, they inspire colleagues to participate actively in DEI efforts.

- **Providing Feedback:** Ambassadors act as conduits for employee feedback, relaying concerns and suggestions to leadership to inform better decision-making.

- **Fostering Accountability:** They help ensure the organization remains aligned with its DEI objectives by holding themselves and others accountable.

3. How to Select and Empower Cultural Ambassadors

- **Identify Passionate Individuals:** Look for employees who naturally advocate for equity and inclusion in their interactions.

- **Provide Training:** Equip ambassadors with the knowledge and tools to promote DEI confidently, including conflict resolution and facilitation skills.

- **Recognize Their Contributions:** Publicly acknowledge ambassadors' roles to reinforce their importance and motivate others to step up.

4. The Ripple Effect of Cultural Ambassadors

When employees witness their colleagues pushing for DEI, they are more likely to participate. Ambassadors generate grassroots support, making DEI initiatives more relatable and compelling. Their influence promotes a sense of shared responsibility, making inclusion a community effort rather than a top-down edict.

From Initiative to Identity

Embedding DEI into an organization's culture requires transforming it from a set of policies and programs into a deeply ingrained value system that guides behavior, decision-making, and interactions at every level. It's about creating an environment where inclusivity becomes second nature—woven into the fabric of daily operations and reflected in how the organization defines its success. While this transformation takes time and sustained effort, the rewards are profound and far-reaching.

A workplace with a strong DEI culture sees benefits in multiple dimensions. Employees feel seen, valued, and respected, leading to improved morale and engagement. This sense of belonging fuels creativity and innovation, as diverse perspectives spark new ideas and solutions. Furthermore, organizations with inclusive cultures enjoy more substantial retention rates, as employees are more likely to stay where they feel appreciated and understood. Beyond internal benefits, a robust DEI commitment enhances the company's reputation, making it a sought-after employer and a respected brand that stands for fairness and opportunity.

The key to achieving this cultural shift lies in intentionality and empowerment. Aligning DEI with the company's culture means embedding these principles into every aspect of the organization, from hiring and training to leadership development and performance evaluations. Leaders must champion DEI as a core value, modeling inclusive behaviors and holding themselves and their teams accountable for upholding these standards.

Cultural ambassadors play a crucial role in this journey. These individuals, drawn from various levels and departments, serve as champions of DEI, driving change from within. They act as connectors, fostering dialogue, identifying areas for improvement, and celebrating progress. By empowering these ambassadors with the tools, training, and support they need, organizations can amplify their DEI efforts and ensure that the message reaches every corner of the workplace.

Ultimately, embedding DEI into the organizational culture is about redefining the company's identity to reflect a commitment to equity and inclusivity. It's not just an initiative or a box to check—it's a way of operating that celebrates the uniqueness of every individual and leverages those differences to drive collective success. Organizations that achieve this transformation become more than workplaces; they become communities where people thrive, grow, and contribute their best.

ADDRESSING INTERSECTIONALITY IN THE WORKPLACE

Addressing intersectionality in the workplace requires a deep understanding of how individual identities intertwine to create unique experiences of privilege, discrimination, and bias. It goes beyond viewing diversity in terms of isolated factors such as race, gender, or religion. Instead, intersectionality recognizes the complexities of human identity, emphasizing that these elements overlap and influence one another in ways that can amplify inequities or advantages.

For instance, the experience of a Black woman in the workplace differs significantly from that of a White woman or a Black man. Her challenges may stem not only from her race or gender but from the combination of both, creating obstacles that are often overlooked by initiatives that treat diversity as a single-layered issue. Similarly, an LGBTQ+ professional with a disability may face compounded barriers that cannot be addressed through policies targeting only one aspect of their identity. These overlapping experiences highlight the necessity of understanding bias in its multifaceted forms.

Creating a workplace culture that embraces intersectionality starts with building awareness and fostering empathy. Education plays a pivotal role in helping employees and leaders understand how their unconscious biases may affect those whose identities are shaped by multiple layers of social and cultural factors. Storytelling and open dialogue allow individuals to connect on a human level, breaking down misconceptions and fostering mutual respect.

Leaders must also commit to creating spaces where all employees feel valued for their authentic selves. This means ensuring policies and practices reflect the diverse needs of intersectional groups, from flexible work arrangements to inclusive hiring criteria. It requires a willingness to listen to underrepresented voices and to actively involve them in decision-making processes. When employees see their unique perspectives acknowledged and celebrated, it fosters a sense of belonging that drives engagement and innovation.

Moreover, addressing intersectionality demands a long-term commitment to equity. Organizations must continually assess their progress, using both data and personal feedback to identify gaps and refine their approaches. It's not just about ticking boxes for representation but creating an environment where every individual feels empowered to contribute and grow.

Ultimately, embracing intersectionality is about acknowledging the rich complexity of human experiences and ensuring that workplaces are equipped to support everyone, regardless of their unique combination of identities. This intentional effort not only enhances inclusivity but also strengthens the organization's collective resilience and creativity. By weaving intersectionality into the fabric of workplace culture, businesses can build a foundation of accurate equity and opportunity for all.

PART VII: SCALING AND EXPANDING DEI INITIATIVES

As businesses expand and function globally, diversity, equality, and inclusion (DEI) take on new dimensions. While the fundamental concepts of DEI remain stable, their application across regions necessitates a nuanced approach. Cultural diversity, community conventions, and local restrictions can significantly influence how DEI efforts are understood and implemented.

Tailoring DEI Strategies to Different Cultural Contexts

A one size-fits-all approach to DEI rarely works in a global setting. What resonates in one culture might be misunderstood or even counterproductive in another. For instance:

- **Understanding Local Norms**

In some cultures, discussing bias is seen as progressive and fosters transparency, while in others, it's considered sensitive or taboo. Organizations must respect these cultural nuances by framing DEI conversations around shared values like fairness and inclusion. Using culturally appropriate language, storytelling, and engaging local champions can help introduce these discussions effectively, ensuring they resonate and build trust across diverse teams.

- **Language Sensitivity**

Words and phrases carry different connotations across languages. Ensuring that DEI messaging is localized and inclusive prevents miscommunication and fosters better understanding.

- **Respecting Cultural Holidays and Practices**: An inclusive workplace acknowledges and accommodates diverse cultural celebrations, dietary preferences, and religious practices. For example, flexible scheduling during Ramadan or providing vegetarian meal options during events can show cultural sensitivity.

Tailoring DEI strategies requires active listening and collaboration with local employees, who can provide invaluable insights into their unique cultural landscapes. When global teams feel that their identities are acknowledged and respected, they are more likely to engage with and support DEI initiatives.

Overcoming Challenges of Implementing DEI in Global Organizations

While the benefits of expanding DEI across global teams are immense, organizations often encounter significant challenges:

- **Balancing Global Standards with Local Flexibility**:

Organizations may have overarching DEI goals, such as achieving gender equity or increasing representation from underrepresented groups. However, the pathways to these goals can differ vastly. For instance, in regions where women face systemic barriers to employment, gender equity initiatives might need to focus on education and recruitment programs. In other regions, the focus might shift to creating policies for career advancement.

- **Navigating Legal and Political Differences**:

Legal frameworks around DEI vary widely. In some countries, anti-discrimination laws are robust and enforceable, while in others, they may be non-existent or poorly implemented. Organizations must work within these frameworks while advocating for inclusive practices.

- **Managing Resistance and Bias**:

Employees in certain regions may resist DEI initiatives due to cultural or societal biases. For example, promoting gender diversity in leadership might be met with skepticism in cultures with traditional gender roles. Education and training programs should address these biases gently yet effectively, emphasizing the benefits of inclusion for individuals and the organization as a whole.

- **Communication and Coordination**:

Implementing DEI initiatives across time zones, languages, and varying levels of digital access can create logistical hurdles. Organizations need robust communication strategies and tools to ensure that all employees feel included in the DEI journey.

Strategies for Success

To overcome these challenges and ensure the success of global DEI initiatives, organizations can:

- **Foster Cross-Cultural Collaboration**: Encourage employees from different regions to work together on DEI projects. This not only enriches perspectives but also builds mutual understanding.

- **Appoint Regional DEI Ambassadors**: Designate local leaders who can champion DEI efforts in their regions. These ambassadors can bridge the gap between global goals and local realities.

- **Invest in Training Programs**: Provide ongoing education on unconscious bias, cultural awareness, and inclusive leadership tailored to specific cultural contexts.

- **Leverage Technology**: Use tools like virtual workshops, multilingual resources, and online collaboration platforms to ensure seamless communication and participation.

The Payoff: A Truly Global Culture of Inclusion

Expanding DEI initiatives across global teams isn't just a moral imperative—it's a strategic advantage. Companies that embrace cultural diversity can tap into a broader range of ideas, perspectives, and talents.

They are better equipped to innovate, adapt, and succeed in a rapidly changing global marketplace.

When DEI strategies are effectively tailored to and embraced by global teams, the organization transcends geographic boundaries. Employees feel valued not just as workers but as individuals, and this sense of belonging drives engagement, productivity, and loyalty.

By addressing cultural differences with respect and intentionality, organizations can build a truly inclusive workplace where diversity isn't just accommodated—it's celebrated.

COLLABORATIVE PARTNERSHIPS AND COMMUNITY ENGAGEMENT

Collaborative partnerships and community engagement are the lifeblood of any successful DEI initiative. Tackling diversity, equity, and inclusion within an organization is a noble effort, but the true power of change lies in expanding these efforts beyond internal boundaries. By joining forces with external organizations—such as non-profits, advocacy groups, and educational institutions—businesses can gain valuable insights, resources, and expertise that they may not possess internally. These partnerships allow organizations to address DEI challenges with a broader perspective, ensuring their strategies are informed by real-world knowledge and experiences.

Take, for instance, a company that partners with an advocacy group focused on empowering women in leadership roles. This collaboration not only enhances the company's internal initiatives but also supports a larger societal goal of closing the gender gap in corporate leadership. Such partnerships create a ripple effect, influencing both the organization and the communities it serves.

Community engagement amplifies this impact even further. When organizations actively participate in the communities around them, they showcase their commitment to creating opportunities and addressing inequities where they are most needed. Imagine a corporation funding scholarships for underserved students or hosting workshops in local schools. These initiatives not only provide immediate benefits to individuals but also lay the groundwork for long-term systemic change.

This outward focus also humanizes DEI efforts. Diversity and inclusion can feel abstract when viewed through the lens of policies and procedures. But when a company's initiatives touch real lives—whether through mentorship programs, volunteer activities, or community outreach—it becomes evident that these efforts are about people, not just metrics.

The beauty of partnerships and community engagement is their capacity to bridge gaps, build trust, and create shared accountability. They remind organizations that DEI is not a solitary journey but a collective one, requiring collaboration, compassion, and a commitment to seeing beyond one's own walls. Through these efforts, change becomes not only achievable but also deeply impactful, extending the values of equity and inclusion far beyond the workplace.

LEVERAGING EXTERNAL FEEDBACK

Creating a truly diverse, equitable, and inclusive (DEI) workplace necessitates more than internal activities; it necessitates listening to people who are directly affected by the existing culture and procedures. External feedback is one of the most powerful tools that organizations may use to better understand their DEI weaknesses and chances for improvement. Using employee surveys, focus groups, and external audits, firms can build a clear, practical route toward significant change.

Using Employee Surveys for DEI Improvement

Surveys offer an efficient and meaningful way to collect diverse feedback from employees, serving as a confidential channel where individuals can share their experiences and challenges without fear of judgment or retaliation. The effectiveness of a survey largely depends on its design, which should aim to uncover insights about inclusivity, fairness, and belonging within the workplace. Thoughtful questions addressing issues like bias, accessibility, and representation can provide a more accurate picture of employee sentiment. Using neutral and open-ended language encourages honest and comprehensive responses, ensuring the data collected is both authentic and actionable.

Anonymity plays a vital role in fostering trust and candor. Employees are far more likely to speak openly when their privacy is safeguarded, which is why many organizations use third-party platforms or anonymized methods to collect responses. This layer of confidentiality ensures that employees feel safe voicing their genuine opinions, leading to more reliable data.

Once the feedback is gathered, careful analysis reveals patterns and recurring themes. These insights can highlight specific areas where the organization may be falling short, such as specific departments or groups feeling excluded or unsupported. Identifying these trends

provides a roadmap for targeted action, allowing leadership to implement changes that address the root causes of workplace challenges. By carefully analyzing survey data and acting on the insights it reveals, organizations can foster a more inclusive and supportive environment for all employees.

Facilitating Focus Groups for Deeper Understanding

Focus groups add depth to survey data by capturing personal experiences and nuanced insights. These moderated discussions create space for employees to share openly, mainly when led by skilled facilitators who ensure a respectful, judgment-free environment.

Including diverse participants enriches the dialogue and prevents bias in representation. Focus groups often reveal subtle issues like microaggressions or barriers to advancement, offering actionable insights for crafting more effective and inclusive DEI initiatives.

Conducting External Audits for Objectivity

An external DEI audit provides an unbiased evaluation of an organization's inclusivity practices, uncovering hidden biases and systemic barriers. Conducted by DEI experts, it examines key areas like hiring, pay equity, and retention using tools like staff interviews and policy reviews. Beyond identifying issues, audits deliver actionable recommendations, such as leadership development for underrepresented groups, helping organizations create a more inclusive and equitable workplace

Incorporating Feedback to Create an Adaptive DEI Strategy

Gathering feedback is just the beginning; the true impact of DEI efforts lies in how organizations act on that feedback. Sharing the findings openly with employees demonstrates transparency and builds trust, showing that their input is valued and taken seriously. However, responding effectively requires strategic prioritization. Not every issue can be addressed at once, so focusing on the most pressing and high-impact concerns—such as pay equity or workplace safety—ensures that meaningful progress is made where it's needed most.

DEI strategies must remain flexible and adaptive, evolving based on ongoing feedback and the outcomes of implemented changes. This iterative approach allows organizations to refine their efforts continuously, addressing what works and what doesn't. Along the way, celebrating achievements—like improved representation or increased employee satisfaction—reinforces the organization's commitment to DEI and keeps the momentum alive. By balancing transparency, prioritization, adaptability, and celebration, organizations can turn feedback into lasting, positive change.

The Human Impact of Listening

When firms actively seek and act on external feedback, employees feel noticed, appreciated, and respected. This promotes loyalty, raises morale, and encourages creativity. Beyond the figures and techniques, there is one simple truth: people flourish in circumstances where they can be heard.

Organizations can develop a DEI strategy that is not only reactive but also proactive, flexible, and deeply based on their employees' requirements. Change begins with listening, and it thrives when action follows.

A VISION FOR THE FUTURE

A vision for the future of diversity, equity, and inclusion (DEI) in the workplace involves more than just addressing the issues of the present—it requires a long-term commitment to creating environments where every employee feels valued and supported. The goal is to build workplaces that are not only inclusive today but remain sustainable and inclusive for generations to come.

Creating such a workplace requires embedding DEI into the very core of an organization's values and mission. This means making inclusion not just a set of policies or a department but a guiding principle that influences every decision made within the company. When DEI is genuinely integrated into an organization's culture, it becomes a part of the daily fabric of how things are done, how people interact, and how business is conducted.

Education plays a crucial role in ensuring that the principles of DEI stay relevant and are acted upon in meaningful ways. Regular training on unconscious bias, cultural awareness, and inclusive leadership helps employees from all backgrounds understand the importance of inclusion and how to combat biases proactively. This type of learning should be a continuous process, not a one-off event, to keep evolving with the times and challenges.

For DEI to endure, there must also be systems of accountability in place. This includes measurable goals and transparent reporting mechanisms to track progress. Accountability ensures that the work is ongoing and that setbacks are addressed, not ignored. In a culture where DEI is prioritized, employees must also feel psychologically safe—meaning they are able to speak freely, challenge the status quo, and share their concerns without fear of judgment or retaliation. A safe, inclusive environment fosters creativity, belonging, and open communication.

Looking further into the future, an inclusive workplace must be adaptable. The challenges and dynamics of tomorrow's workforce will likely be different from those of today. As new technologies emerge and as society continues to evolve, businesses will need to be agile, continuously reevaluating their practices and policies to ensure they are meeting the needs of a diverse and changing workforce. This adaptability allows organizations to stay ahead of trends, creating sustainable DEI practices that withstand the test of time.

In setting long-term goals for DEI and bias reduction, organizations must aim for a holistic transformation. It's not just about achieving quotas or representation goals but also about creating lasting, meaningful changes in how decisions are made and how people are hired, promoted, and developed. This transformation requires organizations to regularly evaluate their systems and processes to identify and eliminate biases that may be embedded in recruitment, leadership, and team dynamics.

The long-term impact of these efforts goes beyond the workplace, too. Companies that embrace DEI principles become pillars of their communities, influencing societal change in meaningful ways. By supporting diverse suppliers, engaging in social justice initiatives, and fostering an overall commitment to equity, businesses can extend their influence beyond their internal operations to create broader societal impact.

The work of creating an inclusive and equitable workplace should be seen as a journey, not a destination. It requires a constant, evolving effort, with each generation of leaders and employees carrying the torch forward. By committing to these principles now, organizations can ensure that the workplace of tomorrow is not only inclusive but also a thriving environment where every individual has the opportunity to succeed. It is this vision—a legacy of inclusion—that will shape the future of the workforce and the world we live in.

CONCLUSION

Unconscious bias quietly shapes the dynamics of workplaces and organizations, often in ways that limit potential and stifle growth. This book has delved deeply into the nature of these biases, explaining their psychological roots and how they manifest in everyday decisions and interactions. Whether in hiring practices, promotions, or team collaborations, these unseen influences create barriers to fairness and equity, undermining both individuals and organizations.

Understanding bias is only the first step. Throughout this journey, we've explored how systemic inequality and historical contexts contribute to its persistence and examined strategies to address it. The path to change requires an intentional and sustained effort to build inclusive practices and create workplaces where everyone can thrive. This isn't a one-time initiative—it's a continuous process demanding self-awareness, structural reforms, and a commitment to accountability.

Organizations that take bold steps to tackle unconscious bias position themselves for success in today's diverse and interconnected world. Diversity and inclusion are more than moral imperatives; they are critical drivers of innovation, creativity, and competitive advantage. Teams that feel valued and empowered bring fresh perspectives, solve problems more effectively, and contribute to an environment of trust and collaboration. Failing to address bias, on the other hand, comes with significant risks, including disengaged employees, reputational harm, and diminished organizational performance.

Both individuals and organizations are responsible for change. Leaders have the power to shape culture by modeling inclusive behaviors, fostering openness, and taking ownership of their actions. Organizations must go beyond surface-level commitments, embedding equity into every layer of their operations and holding themselves accountable for meaningful progress.

While the journey to reducing unconscious bias is complex, it is one worth undertaking. Change begins with recognizing the biases that hold us back and committing to actions that move us forward. The challenges are real, but so are the opportunities to create workplaces where diversity and equity are not only embraced but celebrated. In doing so, we can build environments that empower individuals and organizations to reach their full potential, ensuring that everyone has a fair chance to contribute, succeed, and thrive.

Cheers